More Advance Praise for *Harvesting Intangible Assets*

"A thorough and insightful look back to the future. Andrew J. Sherman has given American business a systematic framework to recapture the innovative and creative energy that built this country. The strength of our nation's future depends on embracing the key principles of *Harvesting Intangible Assets*."

> —Donna Ettenson, Vice President of Operations, Association of Small Business Development Centers

"Growth guru and thought leader Andrew J. Sherman practices what he preaches. When writing *Harvesting Intangible Assets*, he fully leveraged his most valuable intangible assets—his formidable intellect, unrelenting curiosity, and lifetime of diverse business and legal experiences—to deliver a comprehensive, practical road map for business success in our hyper-competitive global markets."

> —Hugh Courtney, Vice Dean, University of Maryland's Robert H. Smith School of Business

"Sherman has laid out a comprehensive road map for harvesting the single most important resource in most companies and countries—its intellectual property. This is a must-read book for every business leader and policy maker."

> —Verne Harnish, CEO of Gazelles; Founder of Entrepreneurs' Organization (EO); and author of *Mastering the Rockefeller Habits*

"Andrew J. Sherman's *Harvesting Intangible Assets* is a cleverly written guide to uncovering hidden revenue in your company's intellectual property that I found especially profound. This book gives you the tools to uncover your creativity and harvest new ideas, strategies, and best practices to ensure success, and Andrew shares his insights in a way that only he can—with humor and style that keeps you wanting more. I highly recommend this read."

> —Parnell Black, MBA, CPA, CVA, NACVA's Chief Executive Officer

"It is rare that you can find 'everything' you want to know about a topic in one place. But if you are looking for the definitive work on all the myriad ways an organization can capitalize on its intellectual property and assets, this is it. *Harvesting Intangible Assets* should be required reading for every CEO."

> —Robert A. Strade, Executive Director and CEO, Entrepreneurs' Organization (EO)

"Intellectual capital is probably the most underutilized resource in most organizations. While many of them spend millions for patents, copyrights, and trade secrets to lock this resource away until its shelf life is expired, Andrew J. Sherman encourages us to seed, 'greenhouse,' grow, mature, and harvest intellectual capital instead. The book is full of practical concepts and insightful examples of companies leading the way to seed ideas to harvest sustainable innovation. I'm sure that this book will be the new *Farmer's Almanac* for the reader on his journey to become an 'intellectual capital' agrarian of the 21st century."

> —Dr. Oliver Schlake, Ralph J. Tyser Teaching Fellow and Senior Executive Education Fellow, Robert H. Smith School of Business, University of Maryland

"Andrew J. Sherman makes a compelling case for assessing, managing, and maximizing intellectual capital, which should—yet often doesn't—account for such a large portion of a company's true value. An enjoyable and important book . . . to be read by today's corporate executives, who should be carefully managing their 'crop' of intellectual capital."

> —Dave Groobert, U.S. General Manager, Environics Public Relations

"In his trenchant new book *Harvesting Intangible Assets*, author, lawyer, and thought leader Andrew J. Sherman reveals for the first time not just how to identify these hidden tools, but also how to fuse them with the specific actions that create competitive advantage. No other work so cogently clarifies the least understood but most valuable aspects of our organizations."

> —T.D. Klein, investor and author of *Built for Change: Essential Traits of Transformative Companies*

"Global thought leader Andrew J. Sherman provides a fresh perspective and looks at intellectual property in a whole new light. Sherman's great new book points out the subtleties of hidden assets and innovation, which could make a world of difference in the life of any company, economy, and society."

> —Sarah Djamshidi, Executive Director, Chesapeake Innovation Center (CIC); President, Maryland Business Incubation

Harvesting Intangible Assets

UNCOVER HIDDEN REVENUE IN
YOUR COMPANY'S INTELLECTUAL PROPERTY

ANDREW J. SHERMAN

AMACOM

American Management Association

New York • Atlanta • Brussels • Chicago • Mexico City • San Francisco
Shanghai • Tokyo • Toronto • Washington, D.C.

Library of Congress Cataloging-in-Publication Data

Sherman, Andrew J.
    Harvesting intangible assets : uncover hidden revenue in your company's intellectual property / Andrew
J. Sherman.
        p.   cm.
    Includes bibliographical references and index.
    ISBN-13: 978-0-8144-1699-0
    ISBN-10: 0-8144-1699-3
    1. Intellectual capital.   2. Knowledge management.   I. Title.
HD53.S495   2011
658.4'038—dc22   2011013154

About AMA

American Management Association (www.amanet.org) is a world leader in talent development, advancing
the skills of individuals to drive business success. Our mission is to support the goals of individuals and
organizations through a complete range of products and services, including classroom and virtual seminars,
webcasts, webinars, podcasts, conferences, corporate and government solutions, business books and research.
AMA's approach to improving performance combines experiential learning—learning through
doing—with opportunities for ongoing professional growth at every step of one's career journey.

Printing number

10   9   8   7   6   5   4   3   2   1

Contents

Contents

✿ Contents

Contents

Preface

There would be no advantage to be gained by sowing a field of
wheat if the harvest did not return more than was sown.
                                        —NAPOLEON HILL

My father's father, Morris Sherman, was a farmer in upstate
New York in the 1930s and 1940s. When health complications
arose in the 1950s that prevented him from working the land,
he took inventory of his intellectual assets, which included deep
knowledge of the regional farming community and strong and
respected relationships with other farmers. He then shifted his
business model to leverage these assets and refocused his attention on the family's farm equipment dealership, which grew each
year for many moons until it was sold at a healthy profit.

The Tao of Morris Sherman is simple—understand the tangible and intangible assets that you have and make the most of
them. It was an obligation that he owed to himself, his family,
and his community. Yet, today, companies of all sizes and in all
industries across our great nation and around the world are

"asleep at the switch" in cultivating, managing, and harvesting critical intangible assets to the detriment of shareholder value and in clear violation of their fiduciary obligations to shareholders, as well as to employees, customers, and society overall.

Why has it taken companies so long to find systems to properly harvest intangibles or recognize the many opportunities that sit just below the strategic surface? Why do so few have effective intellectual asset management (IAM) systems, internal incubators, meaningful R&D budgets, authorized skunkworks operations, corporate venture capital, or customer-driven innovation systems? How can we possibly remain competitive in a global marketplace if we allocate so little time, so few resources, and such low priority to uncovering and fostering innovation and creativity? How long can the significant gaps and disconnects between the universities and government laboratories that *are* investing time in R&D and the larger and smaller companies that have the knowledge and resources to bring products and services to the marketplace continue to exist as billions in research remain underutilized each year? When do we stop talking about the problem and begin solving it? How do we build better communication channels and brands linking sources of capital, sources of innovation, and sources of knowledge in business and market building?

At the company level, how can we better train leaders and managers to more effectively harvest their intangible assets to uncover new opportunities and drive strategies to maximize shareholder value? How do we avoid the waste of critical R&D assets when leadership, priorities, or markets shift? How can we encourage company executives and board members to recognize opportunities that sit right in front of them that they just can't seem to see because they are blinded by short-term fire-fighting priorities and quarter-to-quarter strategic thinking? How do we better foster and reward innovation and creativity internally and externally at all levels in the company?

Harvesting Intangible Assets brings us back to our agrarian roots, but today's crop is intellectual capital. What is old is new and effective again. Today's CEO must build an organization focused on the farming of intellectual assets to uncover hidden revenue opportunities that will make their way to a profitable marketplace in nontraditional channels. Managing the company as an intangible asset farm means that strategic plans will need to be rewritten, mission and values restated, organization charts reexamined, and budgeting and resource allocation decisions revamped. In short, company leaders must be committed to reforming and transforming their companies in the ways that IBM, 3M, Google, and Apple retooled their business models and strategic priorities to drive shareholder value by harvesting intellectual property with a sense of urgency and in pursuit of a significant sense of purpose.

We all need to reconnect with our agrarian roots in the way we build our companies, the way we govern our organizations, and the way we live our lives. The discipline, work ethic, husbandry, stewardship, determination, selflessness, and grit of the world's farmers offer lessons, insights, and values that can make us stronger, more competitive, and better innovators as a society. The cycle of planning, planting, caring, feeding, harvesting, and distributing crops offers a regimen that can guide the innovative process for companies of all sizes and in all industries, as well as in the way we manage our personal affairs.

Farmers learn from an early age how to plant seeds that will yield valuable crops, how to instill discipline in the caring and feeding of those crops, how to weather a storm, and how to establish long-term meaningful and mutually beneficial channel partner relationships and the patience to know that every good harvest is the product of rigor and old-fashioned hard work. They know how to assess whether a market is fertile or barren and would never attempt to grow corn in the desert. They know that a field of crops has no value unless or until it is harvested and brought to the marketplace. There is no "overnight success" or "flash in the pan"—it is a long-term process that requires planning, sweat, prudence, and patience. Instead of living quarter to quarter and robbing shareholders of the long-term horizon that effective innovation truly requires, farmers live from harvest to harvest, from season to season, and from decade to decade in keeping their lands fertile for long-term productivity.

When the markets hit their lows in 2008, it was no surprise that IBM, Google, and Apple maintained triple-digit stock prices. Their commitment to being intellectual capital agrarians was recognized and rewarded by the marketplace while the stock prices of thousands of other companies tumbled into a free fall. The best practices that these companies followed are for the most part public knowledge. The Super Bowl—winning teams opened up significant portions of their playbooks, and few of us took the time or effort to read and understand the plays, let alone try to mold our teams around a commitment to execute them. Shame on us. But it is not too late. It is never too late to pick up your rake and your shovel and begin the strategic farming of your hidden assets. It came as no surprise to me that, nearly 15 years after IBM reshifted its business model away from products and toward strategic consulting, within a span of several months in 2008 and 2009 Dell bought Perot, Xerox bought ACS, and HP bought EDS.

In the face of a deep recession, innovation was viewed by

many companies as a key strategic puzzle piece in driving a recovery. Bringing new products and services to the marketplace was perceived as the *only* way to entice consumers to reach into their badly worn and nearly empty wallets. Making innovation a key element of the branding and marketing campaign was a way to distinguish a company from the rest of an otherwise crowded field. But, from both an inward- and an outward-facing perspective, innovation must be genuine, strategic, well managed, pervasive, and properly rewarded to be effective and to become a component of the company's long-term business model. Innovation that is perceived as shallow, a fad, or a friend that will be short lived is clearly not sustainable and will quickly be exposed as such by both employees and customers. Similarly, innovation that is only barely incremental and is perceived as adding little strategic or tangible value to the target market may be perceived as a hollow attempt at packaging innovation, rather than as a genuine attempt to achieve it. Brand dilution and revenue losses will follow accordingly.

Intellectual capital agrarianism is not limited to technology-centric companies. Sam Walton of Wal-Mart transformed the way in which the world shops, and many others have followed. Charles Schwab pioneered new ways to consume financial services, and many others have followed. Jim Hindman of Jiffy Lube changed the face of automobile repair and maintenance, and many others have followed. Ray Kroc of McDonald's changed the model for restaurant services, and many others have followed. For many companies, precious intellectual assets are like the coins that accumulate under the sofa cushion. Things of value are sitting just under your rear end, but you need to get up and exert some effort to discover them. And you may need to sort through a few old popcorn kernels and lint to find them.

But too many companies have become strategic "couch potatoes," seemingly content to just lay there and watch television as the world passes them by. In December 2009, a *Newsweek* cover story asked, "Is America Losing Its Mojo?" The article observed that innovation and creativity, once as American as apple pie and baseball, are slowly on the decline as we lose ground to developing nations such as China and India and as our nation's youth fall further in the global rankings in key areas such as science, mathematics, and engineering. And the problem is not limited to the United States. In a report published in August 2010 by Professor Colin Coulson-Thomas, only a "handful" of the 60 European companies surveyed by the London-based professor were making effective use of their intellectual capital. His report, titled *Managing Intellectual Capital to Grow Shareholder Value*, concludes that boards of directors must undertake formal reviews of internal policies toward the management of intellectual capital and formulate proactive strategies for harvesting more value from it. Incentives need to be put in place to encourage a stronger culture of innovation.

According to the sixth annual study of corporate innovation spending, 2010 Global Innovation 1000, published by the global management consulting firm Booz & Company, total R&D spending among the world's top spenders on innovation dropped in 2009 for the first time in the 13 years studied. The study revealed that the 1,000 companies that spend the most on research and development decreased their total R&D spending by 3.5 percent to $503 billion in 2009. This followed a relatively strong 2008, during which R&D spending continued to grow despite the recession.

I wrote this book to be the road map, the operations manual, the strategic playbook, and the beacon beam from the lighthouse to lead the way to this transformation and return to our roots. In it, I share my insights, strategies, best practices, and lessons learned from working with some of the world's leading companies, as well as hundreds of small and emerging companies, as a legal and strategic adviser in the areas of intellectual capital harvesting. I have seen the good, the bad, and the ugly. I have seen companies harvest opportunities to create new markets and profit centers and have seen others let valuable assets collect dust and rot to the core.

Our inability to properly harvest our intellectual capital crops has reached a crisis level, with trillions of dollars in shareholder value being wasted. The U.S. Patent and Trademark Office estimates that the intellectual property in the United States alone is worth more than $5 trillion—about two times the annual federal budget—but very few companies are properly harvesting the value for the benefit of their shareholders. Most have simply knowingly or unknowingly failed to commercialize opportunities, resulting in a stale or rotted crop. Others have adapted "scorched earth" policies aimed at confronting and litigating with direct and indirect competitors; these may represent an effective short-term capital-raising exercise but in the long term are likely to be counterproductive, permanently burn potential alliance bridges, and leave the Earth unable to be replanted for many decades. Unless and until we are focused on planting seeds and nurturing the crop of intellectual capital, we will never be competitive in the global marketplace.

Harvesting Intangible Assets is written for companies of all sizes and in all industries, from executives at *Fortune* 1000 companies to leaders of rapid growth entrepreneurial companies. We are *all* farmers and guardians of our company's intellectual assets, and we all owe a fiduciary duty to the stakeholders of our companies to manage and harvest these assets, which may mean cultivating the vision and courage to overhaul our strategic priorities and business models. So grab a pitchfork and put on your metaphorical overalls and join me in the journey that lies in the pages ahead.

Andrew J. Sherman
Washington, D.C.
March 2011

Dedicated to the loving memory of
Morris Sherman,
the Utica agrarian,
and all who follow in his footsteps.

Acknowledgments

The strategies, concepts, issues, and best practices discussed in this book are the result of more than thirty years' experience in serving as a strategic and legal adviser on the harvesting of intellectual capital, from both a legal and a business perspective. It would be impossible to thank all of the people with whom I have had the pleasure of working along the way. The support and loyalty of my many domestic and international clients, as well as my esteemed colleagues at Jones Day, including Steve Brogan, Mary Ellen Powers, Andrew Kramer, John Majoras, Greg Shumaker, Michael Shumaker, Ilene Tannen, Paul Sharer, and Noel Francisco, who all deserve special mention, are much appreciated.

There are certain individuals whose time, hard work, support, and research for this book deserve special mention. I want to thank Professor Oliver Schlake of the Smith School of Business at the University of Maryland for all of his editorial support and encouragement and for his contributions to Chapters 6 and 7, as well as Georgetown University Law Center students Marina Veljanovska and Michael Wolsh for their research support and assistance. We have a dynamic and talented group of global lawyers at Jones Day focused in the areas of intellectual capital harvesting and management, and I am honored to be part of the team. I owe special thanks to my assistant, Jo Lynch, who often serves as my right arm, for her organizational skills and patience.

Robert Nirkind of AMACOM Books was there as always to provide moral and logistical support in pulling this entire project together. He is an excellent orchestrator, editor, and sounding board. I also want to thank Mike Sivilli and Jerilyn Famighetti at AMACOM for their skillful copy editing.

Last, but certainly not least, I am grateful to my wife, Judy, and to my son, Matthew, and my daughter, Jennifer, who once again sacrificed time with me so that I could complete this manuscript. I couldn't ask for a more supportive family.

CHAPTER 1

The Intellectual Capital Agrarian

Never before in history has innovation offered promise of so much to so many in such a short period of time.

—BILL GATES

We are all farmers.

We mark our turf. We protect our property. We plant our seeds. We nurture the soil. We plow our land. We combat adverse weather and ecosystem conditions and overcome adversities. We prepare for our harvest. We carefully remove the frost from the vine. We hope for the best and prepare for the worst as the market sets a price for our efforts. We embrace the notion that our results will be directly tied to our levels of effort and expertise. We begin anew.

No matter what your profession, no matter what your company does, no matter what your life situation may be—we *all* follow this fundamental and deeply rooted agricultural process in some way throughout the days of our lives. We are all the *new* agrarians. But do we recognize ourselves as such? Have we learned from the successes and failures of the agrarian economies that preceded us? Can we learn to apply the traditional as well as the latest best practices of farming to our daily lives and in the growth of our companies? How can we make our lives more enjoyable and enriching and our companies more productive and profitable by adopting an agrarian approach to life planning, time management, resource allocation, innovation harvesting, and business model reshaping?

Consider the following questions as they apply to your life and to your business:

* Have you carefully selected a territory that is fertile for growth and right for your type of crop?

* Do you understand the dynamics of your ecosystem?

* Have you done everything in your power to properly nurture the soil and enhance the land's ability to produce?

* What seeds will you plant, and why?

* Are you ready to invest the time and energy to care for these seeds once planted?

* Whom will you hire to help you raise, harvest, and sell the produce at your farm?

* What tools, resources, and expertise will you require to maximize the fruits of your harvest?

* What adverse weather or market conditions must you overcome to be successful?

* Who else is growing these same crops? How does their experience compare to your own?

* Do you have a keen sense for the cycles and timetables that will optimize your harvest?

* What is your game plan for bringing your crops to the marketplace? Will you do it alone or join with others?

* What are your distribution channels, and who are your target customers? On what basis and criteria will they select your harvest rather than others'? On the basis of price? Quality? Convenience? Availability?

* How will you allocate the revenues that this year's harvest will bring? Have you performed a sensitivity analysis based on high/expected/low target ranges?

* What steps need to be put in place to set the stage for beginning the process again?

* What have you learned from the successes and failures of last year's process to make next year even better?

Each of these questions must be answered by every type of farmer every year in every country around the world. Every year, they "bet the farm," overcoming the challenges of the wind, sun, drought, floods, and other conditions beyond their control to put food on all of our tables. But the questions also apply to *each* of us—in the growth and development of our companies and as applied to the growth and development of ourselves as humans and as an evolving society. And, just as with farming, if we care for the soil and harvest properly, we produce value. If we over-work or overtax the farm and add too many pesticides over too much irrigation, the outputs will be limited and potentially dangerous.

Farmers who strive to perfect this process and to learn from the successes and failures of each year's harvest enjoy financial stability and wealth creation. They work hard to control the variables that are in their power and develop contingency plans around the variables that they can't control. They see the crops as an extension of themselves and are happy as they see them grow and progress. They enjoy the process and connect with the land in a spiritual way. But at the very core and soul of their existence is the relationship between themselves and their land and between their tools and their seeds and between the quality of their harvest and the dynamics of the marketplace.

In building companies and fostering innovation, we must all embrace these same principles. We must put conditions in place that support a corporate culture likely to yield a productive harvest and be constantly planting the seeds of creativity, encouragement, curiosity, empathy, respect, challenge, and fulfillment. We must understand which tools will be most effective for reinforcing the underlying principles of this culture. We must take steps to manage the conditions that are within our control and develop "Plan Bs" for those that we can't. Most important, we must fully invest in the growth and development of our human capital by providing education and training to our teams at *all* levels to teach *how* to become farmers inside our companies and in their own lives.

Time to Market

The agrarian mindset is that there is an ideal and defined window to bring a harvest to the marketplace. If you do it too soon, the product will not yet be ripe. Nobody will buy it. If you're too late, then there will be rotting, spoilage, and waste. Why can't we take the same approach to nonfungible products and services? As shown in Figure 1-1, for every new idea, there is a window of opportunity that parallels the harvest period. Intellectual capital agrarians must be sensitive to these cycles and shifts in market conditions and consumer demand patterns; otherwise, they run the risk of putting shareholder value in peril.

Figure 1-1. The window of opportunity for innovation.

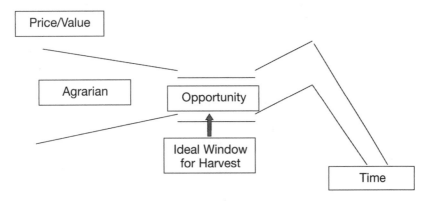

This same window of time can be applied to a technology company's new product or a services firm's timetable for getting a deliverable to a client. Delivery too soon results in a lower value or price because the market is not ready for consumption. Delivery too late will yield stale ideas or be in violation of a client's trust in the relationship by abusing the expected deadline.

Balance Sheets: An Archaic Measure of a Company's True Intrinsic Value

There was a time when, if you needed a "quick" understanding of the net worth of a company, you could examine its balance sheet to determine its assets, subtract the sum of its liabilities, and come up with its net worth. You may have seen a small line item for goodwill to recognize the value of its brand and customer relationships. *But, in today's information-centric and intangible-asset-driven society, looking to the net worth line to determine a company's value would be the strategic equivalent of telling a farmer that the total*

5

value of his farm is limited to the projected wholesale value of the harvestable crops he currently has in the field. Such a valuation methodology would fail to take into account the intrinsic worth of his know-how, his show-how, his distribution channels, his relationship with his team, his land, his future harvests, his systems, his processes, and his leadership skills.

The flaws in our 500-year-old double-entry accounting system for recognizing the value of intangible assets are at the heart of a current and pervasive debate in the accounting and finance professions. At the heart of this debate is NYU Stern School professor Baruch Lev, who has been actively writing and speaking about the flaws in the current GAAP as a way to recognize the true intrinsic assets of knowledge and information-driven companies. Current accounting best practices fail to take into account the dramatic shift in the value-creating functions of today's modern corporations and organizations—most of which are intangible. "Goodwill" is no longer an adequate general utility bucket in which to throw any asset that does not fit neatly into a ledger column.

Lev points out that the problem is significant. He has studied the balance sheets of the Standard & Poor's 500—500 of the largest companies in the United States, many of which are not in high-tech industries. The market-to-book ratio of these companies—that is, the ratio between the market value of these companies and the net asset value of the company (the number that appears on the balance sheet)—is now greater than 6 to 1. What this means is that the balance-sheet number—which is what traditional accounting measures—represents only 10 percent to 15 percent of the true intrinsic and strategic value of these companies. Even if the stock market is inflated, even if you chop 50 percent off the market capitalization, you're still talking about a huge difference between value as perceived by those who pay for it day to day and value as the company accounts for it.

Another example: John Kendrick, a well-known economist who has studied the main drivers of economic growth, reports that there has been a general increase in intangible assets contributing to U.S. economic growth since the early 1900s: in 1929, the ratio of intangible business capital to tangible business capital was 30 percent to 70 percent, but in 1990, the ratio had shifted to 63 percent to 37 percent, and it continues to shift as we evolve deep into the information age.

The most relevant information to managers and investors concerns the enterprise's value chain. By value chain, I mean the fundamental economic process of innovation that starts with the discovery of new products, services, or processes, proceeds through the development and the implementation phase of these discoveries and establishment of technological feasibility, and culminates in the *commercialization* of the new products or services. Lev recommends that GAAP include a "Value Chain Blueprint," a measure-based information system for use in both internal decision making and disclosure to investors that reports in a structured and standardized way about the innovation process.

Lev also recommends that current financial accounting practices evolve around our intellectual-capital-driven society. The broad denial of intangibles as true assets detracts from the quality of information provided in the balance sheet. Even more serious is its adverse effect on the measurement of earnings. The matching of revenues with expenses is distorted by front-loading costs by the immediate expensing of intangibles and recording revenues in subsequent periods unencumbered by those costs. For example, as R&D projects advance from formulation through feasibility tests (such as alpha and beta tests of software products) to the final product, the uncertainty about technological feasibility and commercial success continually decreases. Accordingly, Lev proposes that accounting recognize as assets all intangible investments with attributable benefits that have passed certain prespecified technological feasibility tests. Managers should develop the capability to assess the expected return on investment in R&D, employee training, information technology, brand enhancement, online activities, and other intangibles and compare these returns with those of physical investment in an effort to achieve optimal allocation of corporate resources. Today, most business enterprises do not have the information and monitoring tools required for the effective management of intangible assets.

The Tomato Exercise

If instead of selling _____ (whatever business you are in), how would your business model, windows of opportunity, and distribution channels change if your product were tomatoes? You might consider these points:

* How long will it take to produce a tomato from seedling to young roots to harvest?

* How long do you have to get it to the marketplace once it is picked? How will it arrive?

* At what point is it too soon to present this tomato to the marketplace? At what point is it too late?

* Will the tomato be sold as fresh produce at a local supermarket? Or at an organic grocer? How will this affect your time to market?

* What steps will you need to take to grow tomatoes out of season?

* Or might it be canned, pickled, or processed into a sauce or salsa? If so, how will your buyers and channels differ? How will your pricing model change?

Now apply the lessons learned from the tomato exercise to your own company's business model. How could it be improved or modified? Is there a component to your current business model that is more subject to spoilage, waste, or timetable sensitivities that you may realize? Is there a timetable that you have assumed or taken for granted that is actually inconsistent or misaligned with the needs or expectations of your current or target clients or customers? Is there a way to protect and preserve the idea from an early death if it is not quite ripe (such as intellectual capital and innovation "greenhousing," where the concept is put into a safe environment until it is ready to withstand "outdoor weather conditions")? And how have the past ten years of communications technology influenced or compressed these timetables?

In the professional services businesses, as an example, client expectations have shifted around the personal digital assistant (PDA) society. We are expected to be more responsive, more succinct, and more efficient, all on a 24/7 basis. What would have "spoiled a tomato" in 1998 is not the same window of opportunity or window of tolerance or window of reasonable expectation that it is in 2011. Getting back to a client with an answer in a few days is no longer acceptable; those few days have become a few hours at most and have further evolved into a few minutes. Tomatoes must be seeded, grown, harvested, and delivered as ideally ripe for eating in a much compressed window. And if you can't keep up, your customers will find a farmer who will meet their timetable needs without sacrificing quality. Today's new agrarian must figure out ways to apply principles of ripeness, spoilage, and shelf life to the harvesting of intellectual capital, knowledge, ideas, innovation, solutions, connections, access, relationship building, and the provision of advice and guidance.

Our shift to a services-driven, knowledge-based, and technology-enabled economy has not affected the *value* of the principles of agrarianism, but it has changed the nature of the deliverable and compressed the timetable for delivery. This is especially true in a culture and a society where consumers can select from an abundant inventory and can often dictate the prices and terms upon which they will choose to consume. Our younger generations have been trained to expect quality on an immediate basis and at a fair price—and served up in a manner that is consistent with their core values. These are principles that have enabled companies such as Chipotle, Best Buy, Jiffy Lube, Five Guys, and Netflix to grow at such a rapid pace to the detriment of their competitors. This new generation of consumer has also been considered to be in a position to influence the assembly and design of the product and its features. Look at the works of James Surowiecki, author of *The Wisdom of Crowds*, and Jeff Howe's article in the June 2006 issue of *Wired* magazine, "The Wisdom of Crowds," for additional information on this phenomenon. The key point to understand is that the consumer is often better equipped to influence and make decisions in real time than even the most extensive market research.

We have gone from a society where Burger King proclaims "hold the pickle, hold the lettuce, special orders don't upset us" to building your sandwich or burrito as you move your way across the counter formats found at Subway or Chipotle. Today's intangible asset agrarian must put communication channels in place— typically via focus groups, dynamic customer service and relationship management practices, and social networking tools—to allow its target consumer to influence innovation and play a role in the decisions and outcomes. Those that can't adjust or don't care will be raising crops that will surely spoil.

This is also the same generation that seems to always "has to have" the latest and greatest technology with the newest bells and whistles, thereby compressing the window for incremental innovation and new product development but also shortening the cycle of product replacement, creating additional consumption and cross-selling opportunities for service plans, warranty sales, training, and support. The amount of time that an average consumer is willing to hold on to a computer, a cell phone, a PDA, or even a vehicle that does not offer the latest features and capacities continues to be compressed, even in a weakened economy. This established phenomenon presents both opportunities and challenges for the new agrarian, who is forced to cultivate, innovate, and promulgate new products and services faster, better, and cheaper but who will be rewarded by greater demand and more frequent purchase cycles if he can adjust and deliver. And these agrarian lessons that appear to be most easily applicable to the consumer electronics or automobile industries actually extend to many other significant pockets of the economy, from health care to financial services, from professional services to home repair, and from maintenance to education and publishing. We can all learn from this paradigm shift and can all be better and more efficient farmers, regardless of our underlying crops.

Challenges for the New Agrarian

A commitment to being an agrarian of intellectual capital requires a vision to redefine and transform the traditional ways that business has been conducted. Innovation includes new approaches, new business models, new channels, new value propositions, new pricing, new packaging, and new marketing and branding strategies. There must be a willingness to challenge the "way things have always been done" with a healthy disregard for the norm as part of a quest to make things better, more desirable, more marketable, more efficient, and more profitable. The variables of branding, quality, positioning, packaging, nutrient-adding, and flavoring all helped lead a generation that drank water from a faucet to purchase, in 2010, more than $80 billion of bottled water that featured carbonization, flavors, caffeine, minerals, vitamins, herbs, and sweeteners.

Not all innovation is breakthrough and life changing, but it often can provide new product lines, new services, new revenue streams, and new profit centers for companies of all sizes. Forty years ago, Bernie Sadow, an entrepreneur based in Massachusetts whose business made luggage and carts, had the simple idea of adding wheels to the bottom of a suitcase. He filed for a patent in 1970 and helped change the way we all travel. Dunkin' Donuts for years wasted the dough that filled the center of its donuts until it realized that consumers would buy them; the rest is history. Zipcar made a slight shift in the car rental business model and met the needs of the urban dweller in launching its now world famous car-sharing service—without really "inventing" anything new except how customers would interact with its inventory. Similarly, it may be hard to believe, but 1 out of every 12 Americans now owns a Snuggie, which comes in 15 different styles. As a television-driven success story, the Snuggie—a low-innovation, marketing-driven phenomenon that essentially combines a blanket and a bathrobe—joined the Clapper and the Pocket Fisherman in the "when we see it, we want to buy it" hall of fame.

More recently, we have seen perhaps the ultimate marketing innovation: goods that required little innovation to their core product. In the fall of 2010, for example, automakers launched a campaign to make the minivan cool again. Toyota's "Swagger Wagon" advertisements featured a suburban couple rapping hip-hop style about the coolness of their mom-mobile, and sales increased by more than 20 percent. In December of that same year, the Hartford insurance company ran a television commercial that featured a handcrafted Western boot maker's daughter who suggested that his same designs and materials could be used for a new line of women's handbags and the microbrewer's employee who took a few bottles of beer home to serve as the base for bread batter and subsequently baked goods that have become a core component of the product menu of the company. And, in January 2011, PepsiCo launched a campaign to "snackify" some of its most popular beverages, essentially launching line extensions around its Tropicana, Odwalla, and Yoplait brands into smoothies, energy boosters, and brown-bag snacks.

These are all examples of ideas that transformed into products, with very little need for significant investment in research and development or expensive market testing or consumer adoption. They were *truly* coins under the sofa cushion—just a few minutes of some out-of-the-box thinking from those closest to your business model (the employees) and the results can be a quality product and a willing and already loyal consumer.

The challenges to this business model or relationship transformation are as follows:

* **Getting consumers to start paying for something that is actually (or that they perceive should be) available to them at no cost.** How does a business start charging for something that it typically has been giving away? How can you

13

build a business upon a platform that is public knowledge or owned by the whole? Well, it happens more often than you may realize. Take, for example, the Internal Revenue Code, a long and detailed body of rules that is available for anyone to buy, read, and learn at any time. The core knowledge is public information—interpretation, guidelines, best practices, and so on—that has fueled income opportunities for accountants, lawyers, consultants, training companies, and publishers for more than 100 years (see Figure 1-2). *Just because the core knowledge is available does not mean you can't create value-added services models around it.*

As demonstrated in Figure 1-2, even core knowledge that is available at no cost to the general public has layers of intellectual capital and expertise that can be leveraged into viable, sustainable, and profitable business models.

* **Getting consumers to pay for something that you have been giving away for free (to date).** We all know that it is never easy to start charging people for something that you have been traditionally giving to them for a long time at no cost. It is likely to go over about as well as charging your children rent when they come home to live with you after college. But, after some initial kicking and screaming, they will adjust their thinking and adjust to the new paradigm of the relationship, *but only if* you redefine the value proposition in a way that helps them see the light. Louis V. Gerstner Jr. had this same problem when he became CEO of IBM in 1993. For many years, executives, managers, and field support teams had essentially been giving away their knowledge to customers at no charge with the hope of selling and supporting hardware. A significant body of knowledge related to computer system design, industry applications, customized processes, training, and support had been accumulated that was routinely provided as part of customer sales and support. Gerstner

Figure 1-2. The intellectual capital matrix of ownership.

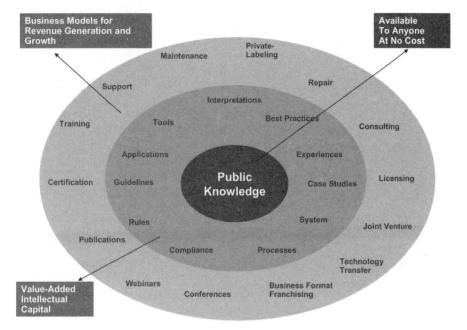

had the vision to realize that the value of these services and the harvesting of this intellectual capital were potentially more valuable and more profitable than the sale of hardware. He was right. In 2009, IBM enjoyed consulting revenues of more than $95 billion, and it is one of the world's largest consulting firms in dozens of industry vehicles. It takes vision, courage, persistence, patience, and fortitude to transform your business models in a manner that takes a page out of the IBM playbook—but in a knowledge-driven and services-based global economy, that may be exactly what you must do to survive and thrive.

* **Getting consumers to pay (again) for something that technology has liberated—legally or illegally.** The impact of the Internet and the rise of Web 2.0 and social networking have been significant on many levels. They have forced many industries to significantly rethink, reform, and transform their business models in order to bring a paying customer back to a relationship that they may have left because market or technological conditions have changed.

The publishing industry, for example, has been forced to redefine its value proposition to consumers who were happy to pay for books, magazines, and newspapers until that same knowledge was available on demand at a moment's notice on a device the size of a credit card. It is not easy to expect a consumer to pay a monthly subscription fee to a publication that is stale by the time it arrives at your doorstep. Many such efforts have failed. Those products that have survived have leveraged and strengthened their boards and transformed their business models. *They embraced the technology as their friend instead of loathing it as their enemy.*

* **Getting consumers to pay for the "new and improved" when the existing product still works well.** How do you get a consumer to replace a product that meets its needs with the new and improved version before the existing product runs its natural life cycle? Well, back to our friends at Apple for some insights. The initial iPod was plain white and had storage capacity of 5GB. That worked well, and millions were sold. But then the iPods in different colors, sizes, storage capacities, and features trickled their way into the market, and everyone *had* to have the latest version, even if the old unit worked perfectly fine. I was viewed as a dinosaur by my family when I did not have an iPod that played video or that was not lime green. Suddenly we had four humans in one household and nine different iPods in many different colors, sizes, and shapes, as well as all of the accessories (e.g., players, carrying cases, headphones) that went with them. And then came the iPhone and now the top-selling iPad, and who knows what's next? Suddenly a company that primarily sold its computers to graphic designers and nerds had transformed its brand to become the dominant in-house and mobile technology provider in the world. How can your company learn from this experience? How can you be an agrarian of your intellectual capital and transform the shape, sizes, uses, perceptions, models, and subtle messaging that currently define your brand and customer value proposition?

Many industries face this same challenge, from consumer electronics companies to automobile manufacturers to apparel makers to home appliances manufacturers to furniture manufacturers to office equipment vendors. Why should I buy a new television when the one I have works perfectly fine? Why should I buy a new car when the one I have still gets me to work and back every day? Why should I buy that new suit when I have ten suits in my closet that still fit well? Why should I replace our copier or conference room table when they still seem to be functional and meet our needs? Consumers' willingness to upgrade, enjoy new features and benefits, stay in line with the current trends, embrace advanced technology, and step outside their comfort zone has allowed the fashion, electronics, and furniture industries to survive. Being an intellectual capital agrarian means that you are committed to being close enough to your consumer to truly understand *how* and *why* they consume and to help them understand *why* they should consume *differently* and more *frequently*.

We require food several times a day to survive, but we have many choices as to what to eat, where to eat, what to pay, and what to experience, and we all know what tastes and flavors we like and dislike. When our target consumer can potentially consume our product several times a day, the key challenges are positioning and differentiation. But, when our target consumer may interact with us only once every five years or longer, the key challenges become finding a way to redefine the consuming pattern and seeking recurring revenues.

A good example of this is the pharmaceutical industry. With the costs of drug research and FDA approvals through the roof, many companies have dwindling pipelines and rely on key products whose patents are expiring. The growth of the generic industry (which can produce those products after patents expire) has forced large companies to embrace branding as a key strategy to drive shareholder value (hence the increase in television advertising for prescription and nonprescription drugs over the past seven years). Well-known brands such as Sudafed and Zantac have had to transform from the monopolistic world of "by prescription only" to a more brand-driven competitive environment where customer's perceptions of their medications matter as much as the actual results.

* **Getting consumers to pay for a new way of packaging and building on consuming individuals and components that already exist and are already available.** I am willing to bet the price of this book that most of its readers have never heard of a compilation copyright. The beauty of this type of intellectual capital is that property rights and value attach to the compiler, the assembler, the organizer, the refiner, and the publisher. You do not need to actually *create* the individual parts, but you are rewarded for the creativity and value that went into creating the sum of the parts.

For example, 50 exabytes (150 billion gigabytes) worth of data were created in 2005. In 2010, we created more than 1,200 exabytes, a nearly ten-fold increase in a short five years. By 2013,

Cisco estimated that the amount of traffic flowing over the Internet annually will exceed 667 exabytes, so nearly half of all information created will be shared. Nearly 16 petabytes of new information are generated each day, and more than 80 percent of these data are unorganized, unstructured, unfiltered, and unusable—unless and until value-added driven companies help us organize, optimize, analyze, and store all of this information. The vast potential of this data deluge is just beginning to be harvested, and new types of data agrarians are being birthed every week. Creating data reports, aggregating, optimizing, and interpreting are all protectable rights and valuable services protected by compilation copyright and, to a lesser extent, trade secret law. Again, you do *not* have to be the author or creator of the data, but you *do* have to find ways to mine for the diamonds in the rough and then present those gems to the marketplace in a manner in which customers will be willing to consume and benefit from them. Business intelligence, data mining, knowledge management, and data storage are all rapidly growing industries.

The data deluge has already enabled, empowered, and improved a wide variety of industries, but there is still a long way to go. Credit card and insurance companies crunch through billions of transactions and claims to identify fraudulent claims, unauthorized uses of credit card and Social Security numbers, and other forms of waste and abuse. Retailers use data mining to manage inventory and to custom-tailor sales and promotions to their customers' needs, wants, and consuming patterns. Security agencies are data-mining social networks and blogs to find active communities and their outliers that are prone to terrorism or different acts related to national security. Businesses create recommendation systems for online stores that recommend products to Internet visitors on the basis of the results of mining the customer's personal Web logs and even hire people to write reviews, drive people to other sites, and raise online brand awareness.

* **Getting consumers to consume that have never consumed before.** A recent McKinsey study estimates that there will be 975 million new middle-class households added to our planet over the next 20 years. The consuming power of these households will increase threefold, from $3 billion to $9 billion, over time. For these consumers, the entire concept of disposable or discretionary income will be new as their consuming patterns shift from *needs* to *wants*. Intellectual capital agrarians will need to develop and implement innovative products, services, pricing models, and distribution channels to reach these new consumers, who will be empowered to spend and make decisions regarding the allocation of their modest wealth that their previous generations have never experienced. Understanding how and why they will choose one product over another will be critical to business growth at all levels and in most industries.

A Commitment to New Agrarianism

Farmers have had to reinvent themselves for centuries. As weather patterns, challenges, demand shifts, or commodity prices fluctuate, farmers retrain their systems and replant their soil to grow different crops within the parameters of their core skills and the capabilities of their fields and use external resources such as pesticides and fertilizers to help manage and mitigate their risk of failure. So, too, must companies around the globe. In the past 20 years, the impact and presentation of digital media have forced major industries such as film, music, publishing, hospital-

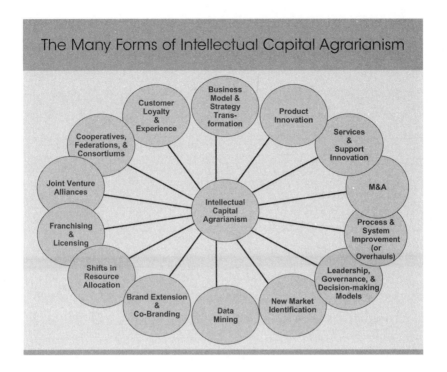

The Many Forms of Intellectual Capital Agrarianism

Intellectual Capital Agrarianism

- Business Model & Strategy Transformation
- Product Innovation
- Services & Support Innovation
- M&A
- Process & System Improvement (or Overhauls)
- Leadership, Governance, & Decision-making Models
- New Market Identification
- Data Mining
- Brand Extension & Co-Branding
- Shifts in Resource Allocation
- Franchising & Licensing
- Joint Venture Alliances
- Cooperatives, Federations, & Consortiums
- Customer Loyalty & Experience

ity, and airlines and automobile manufacturing to redefine and reinvest themselves—both internally and outwardly—to their customers. Some will survive and adapt, and others will be left behind. The leaders and governors of these companies can either talk or act, predict or invest, ignore or embrace, or be dismayed or invigorated by these challenges and grim realities. The marketplace will reward the new agrarians who build on their core to redefine, re-create, reseed, and reharvest their crops on the basis of changes in the market.

We have reached a crossroads in our evolution and in our society where business model transformation has replaced traditional business model planning. Business moves at the speed of light, and those still pedaling bicycles to reach their customers will be left behind. The pace at which changes need to be made have gotten much faster, and the consequences of ignorance or stubbornness have become much more severe. A commitment to being a company driven by innovation, creativity, and intellectual capital agrarianism is no longer an option; it is mandatory for survival and a requirement for thriving. Technological and business-model dinosaurs have joined their prehistoric brethren models at the pearly gates of what was, rather than what is or what will be.

Innovation triumphs over complacency at every turn and in every industry. Wal-Mart grows to nearly $450 billion in global revenues while Circuit City, Eddie Bauer, 800 Mattress, Comp USA, Ritz Camera, and Filene's Basement filed for bankruptcy in 2009. Apple and RIM thrive, while Nokia and Motorola struggle to redefine themselves in a market that seems to have shifted almost overnight. There were more than 5 billion songs downloaded on iTunes by June 2009, just as Tower Records closed its last retail store. Amazon continues to expand its range of products and consumers as Barnes & Noble and Borders struggle to fill their large stores with enough customers to survive; in the ultimate "tipping point," in the second quarter of 2010, Amazon announced that, for the first time, its e-book sales exceeded its hardcover book revenues. Facebook hit 300 million users by September 2009 as AOL celebrates its 30th anniversary but has a subscriber based that peaked at 30 million in 2003 but numbered fewer than five million in 2010, when the number of global Facebook users hit 500 million. There are lines out the door for a fresh, handmade Chipotle burrito, while units at Fatburger, Sbarro's, Red Lobster, Applebee's, and Outback seemed to be closing by the day. Nobody is immune to change and the mandate to innovate. Even venerable growth companies such as

Starbucks and Nike and Disney have had to restate and recalibrate their value proposition to their once fiercely loyal and profitable customer base. In fact, in January 2011, Starbucks changed its logo and dropped the word "coffee" while increasing the prominence of the stylized mermaid as it evolves toward a broader product line and an expanded packaged-goods business. If Starbucks can evolve beyond coffee in its name, what message does that send to the rest of us?

CHAPTER 2

Planting the Seeds: Fostering a Culture of Innovation

Imagination is more important than knowledge. Creativity is more important than expertise.

—ALBERT EINSTEIN

Ask any farmer of any crop whether it is possible to produce a bountiful and profitable harvest from land that is barren or overworked, with seeds that are stale, with animals that are malnourished, with a team that is incompetent, or with tools that are ineffective, and you will get a blank stare reserved only for us special "city folk." Farmers have known for centuries what it takes to produce a bumper crop and what conditions and variables will either enhance or derail this process. With limited resources, staff, and window of opportunity, they put the wheels into motion at the start of each agricultural cycle to ensure a profitable output and navigate through adversities and hurdles to their productivity.

So why, then, if our farming brothers and sisters have known this to be true for 500 or 600 years, do leaders of companies and their boards continue to scratch their heads in wonderment at the lack of creativity, innovation, and new product and service pipelines when they are sitting atop companies that are attempting to plant creative seeds into a culture that is barren, a reward system that is broken, a leadership that is blind, a channel that is disloyal, innovation teams that are getting mixed signals, and engineers and scientists who are being implored to innovate without the appropriate tools, resources, budgets, organizational structure, systems, protection strategies, cultural support, or reward systems? No farmer in his right mind would attempt to grow crops under these conditions, nor should any forward-thinking CEO should attempt to innovate or harvest intellectual capital in such an environment.

W. Edwards Deming once observed that, in most companies, a small percentage of employees are clearly superior, a small percentage are incompetent, and the majority of the remaining people will perform as well as the organizational systems and processes *allow them to do so*. Deming goes on to observe that one of the two primary roles of leadership, then, is to continually cultivate and improve these systems and processes to motivate and incent people to perform at their peak, thereby driving shareholder value. The phrases "if it ain't broken, don't fix it" and "if you keep doin' what you're doin', then you'll keep gettin' what you're gettin'" are the antithesis of Deming's continuous improvement model. To drive this point home, some define insanity as doing the same thing over and over again and expecting it to produce different results.

To build and sustain a culture truly committed to creativity, innovation, and intellectual capital agrarianism, boards of directors and executives of companies of all sizes and in all industries must break through the management paradigm of insanity. Turf wars, politics, red tape, budget nepotism, envy, ego, greed, cronyism, short-term thinking, and rapid changes in strategic direction for no apparent reason must be removed from the culture and replaced with the fuel, the tools, the resources, and the attitudes that drive the innovative process. Any organization, whether a for-profit business, a nonprofit organization, a government agency, or an academic institution, that has a culture where there is a direct or indirect, explicit or implicit, stated or whispered vested interest in keeping things exactly the same to produce continuity and to win the elusive prize of job security will surely die a slow death and will never be a place where creativity is cherished or innovation is harvested. Cultures of innovation are places where creativity is celebrated, rewarded, and cherished at all levels in the organization. When teams are truly inspired and passionate about their work, they are much more likely to discover and to dream without the fear of "extra effort" or discretionary time (e.g., time and effort expended in the workplace beyond what is typically expected) that innovation can flourish and valuable crops can grow.

Initiatives to foster innovation and creativity must be *both* top-down and bottom-up. From a top-down perspective, the chairman/CEO/founder/visionary plays a significant role in establishing innovation priorities, resource allocation, and project timetables. Anyone who has worked for either large or small companies understands that when a CEO or founding entrepreneur is driven to accomplish something, everyone in the organization seems to find a way to get it done. But the bottom-up side of the equation is more challenging. New ideas generated by those who are new to the company or at the bottom of the corporate ladder are not as likely to come to fruition *unless* systems are in place to allow the project to make its way onto a decision maker's desk and *unless* the culture of the company is truly open and encouraging to innovation at all levels of the institution. Ideas at the bottom of the food chain will die an early death if the pathway to resource allocation is fraught with dozens of speed bumps and brick walls. Management structures and systems that foster these barriers are demotivating and demoralizing and not likely to develop the creative "bench strength" that a company needs to sustain long-term innovation. Similarly, such a culture is not likely to be attractive to many members of the "Gen-Y" population, who favor being engaged and empowered early on in their careers.

The commitment to innovation cannot be random or episodic. Your strategy cannot be to sit around and wait for the next "flash of creative genius." There must be a balance between the time, attention, and resources devoted to the company's more established "cash cows" that generate durable and predictable revenue streams and the development of the potentially highly productive and profitable products for the future. Leaders of the company must create, empower, encourage, mentor, and reward internal catalysts, mavericks, and creativity champions who are not afraid to take chances and who have the skill sets to think/see/act differently in spite of organizational barriers. It is critical that all employees, especially those who are expected to innovate as a part of their core job description, understand where they fit into the culture of creativity, how they will be rewarded, and why it is critical to the future and prosperity of the organization and its stakeholders. The development and strengthening of human capital must be at the forefront of the CEO's "burning" agenda, and internal pioneers must be given enough clout and adequate resources to succeed or fail. Be clear in communicating the systems that will reward performance beyond expectations, but avoid rewarding employees for merely doing what is already part of their basic job description—it is bad enough that we have fostered a "trophy generation" of young people who expect a gold star for a C+ report card.

Reward systems vary from company to company. Try different methods, and talk to your constituents to see what will be the source of the greatest motivation. Some systems provide basic monetary bonuses, others use "frequent flyer" point systems that can be redeemed for rewards, others offer more "venture capital"– style rewards offering percentages of sales or profits, and a few companies have tried to create "priceless" awards, like dinner with the CEO or a one-month use of his VIP parking space or driver. But, at the core of any motivation system that will actually yield results must be a genuine passion for the work and a heartfelt desire to contribute to the advancement and growth of the company. If the psychological commitment to innovate is missing, all the cruises to the Caribbean will be meaningless and a waste of corporate resources. In fact, many inventors cite the need to express themselves, to leave a legacy, to remove a chip on their shoulders, or to enjoy the simple pleasures of collaboration and interaction with others as their primary motivation for innovation, All these ranked ahead of economic reward.

We know the simple rules for what we need to do to improve innovation and intellectual capital harvesting; we just need to *actually* do it on a sustainable and consistent basis. The mystery lies *not* with the what or the how *but* with the when and the who. In May 2010, IBM (which has been a research pioneer in the fostering and harvesting of innovation) released a CEO study on creating an innovative culture. CEOs were asked what they were looking for in middle-level and upper-level managers and leaders to help increase innovation inside their companies. Characteristics cited include those who can "embrace ambiguity," "take risks that disrupt legacy business models," and "leapfrog beyond tried-and-true management styles." CEOs surveyed named creativity as the single most important attribute needed in their leadership teams. Wow. Sounds exciting and promising. Where do I sign up?

If I sound cynical, it is not because the IBM study was flawed. In fact, quite the contrary. I have no doubt that these CEOs answered honestly and truly believe in their hearts that these traits are hypercritical. *The real question is: who else got the memo?* Have these traits found their way into the position descriptions, the interview questions, and the screening techniques used by the human resources (HR) department? Has the CFO worked with HR to create financial (and, of course, nonfinancial, which can be equally if not more important) rewards and incentives to foster more creativity and innovation? Have budgets been allocated to provide the tools and resources needed to innovate? Have the communication silos been broken down to ensure collaboration and cooperation both inside and outside the company? Have expectations for productivity been adjusted (as they have at 3M and Google) to allow time in the workday for creativity and breakthrough thinking? Have egos and norms been put in check long enough for management to truly listen to new ideas and strategic alternatives? Have those who are rewarded when things remain exactly the same been removed or demoted within the organization? Have those affected by changes in the business model (e.g., customers, suppliers, vendors, sources of finance) been informed and considered (impact analysis)?

Building a Genuine Culture of Innovation

An organization truly committed to innovation is not afraid to ask "Why?" and then carefully listen to the answers. It is not afraid to ask "How?" and then follow the pathways that are recommended. It is not afraid to ask "Who?" and then make the hard decisions about the staffing of projects and new initiatives or an overhaul of the organizational charts and fiefdoms that go with the little boxes. It always asks, "What if?" and then takes the time to carefully consider the possibilities. It is not afraid to sit down with teams of employees or customers or vendors or suppliers and ask: "If you had the power to change anything that we do, what would it be? What really, really bothers you? How can we change it?"

When people start answering these questions openly and honestly, without self-interest, cronyism, or hidden agendas, and leaders listen and carefully consider and evaluate the answers, also without self-interest or hidden agendas, the seeds of an innovative culture have truly begun to be planted. The converse is equally true—*until* this happens, no culture of innovation can be built.

Leadership and Governance Principles for Fostering a Culture of Innovation

A culture of innovation begins at the top but must permeate and trickle through all levels and all functions within any organization. The work ethic, transparency, simplicity, humility, integrity, and accountability of most farmers offer insights and leadership lessons for all of us, particularly leaders interested in fostering a culture committed to intellectual capital agrarianism. Norms must be put into place and enforced that foster cooperation, teamwork, candor, a sense of a common purpose, and a commitment to a set of institutional core values that transcends individual agendas and priorities. These shared values must be truly embraced by everyone, not just appear on a page on the company's website. People are more likely to innovate and truly want to improve their workplace when they identify with and want to be governed by a set of shared institutional and consistent values and when they are confident that the fruit of their innovation labors are aligned with overall companywide strategies and goals. The Wal-Mart cheer is not just a set of words recited with enthusiasm at company meetings. It represents a bonding and a connection with the company's roots and the values and vision of its founder, Sam Walton, long after his passing.

Governance in a culture of intellectual capital agrarianism must strike that delicate balance between enforcing candor and removing the fear of failure. Fear is the enemy of innovation. When a culture punishes failure, then people work toward maintaining the status quo, and no headway is made. At the other extreme, in a company still being run like an elementary school classroom, where everyone is so "nice" that candor is discouraged out of a desire to avoid "ruffling anyone's feathers" or "upsetting the apple cart," projects that should have been sunsetted years earlier are allowed to continue in perpetuity, costing the shareholder's time, money, and lost opportunity.

A good leader is successful in fostering clear and friendly

interdepartmental communication. Enormous value is lost when a company's different parts do not talk to each other or use the same language. The scientists and idea developers must be able to clearly communicate to the business leaders and those in the marketing and government affairs departments. R&D managers must acquire business skills in order to convey their ideas properly, and policy and business makers must be able to understand R&D's scientific reasoning. This is important, not only because it protects against costly lawsuits related to product malfunctioning and rushed deadlines imposed by the business departments that put profits before safety as urged by the scientists but also because innovation, creativity, and potential business opportunities will be lost forever if employers don't feel comfortable sharing them.

Those who excel at generating ideas must be paired with those who can shape it and mold it into a profitable product or service. Birthing an idea is *not* the same as raising a healthy and well-balanced product or service. It takes a village of coaches, supporters, champions, facilitators, designers, marketers, resource margins, and analysts throughout the hierarchy of the organization to bring strong ideas to fruition and to discard or put on the back burner those that either are not ripe or are incapable of maturing into a viable product or service (or at least incapable of doing so within the four walls of *this* particular organization, which is where licensing or partnering become strategically relevant). Innovation is meaningless without implementation and strategy, and those who implement cannot function without an initial vision. Successful cultures driven by innovation make these two realities interdependent, and both sets of efforts are nearly equally rewarded.

An effective innovation-minded leader will train both types

of employees in the skills they are lacking, create proper channels of communication, and foster a friendly environment where every employee feels free to contribute to the discussion. Part of 3M's success over the years is attributable to its transformation of its IT department from a back-office support role to a strategic business partner. 3M expanded its executive management team by including IT leaders, thereby making it easier for IT staff to share their vision and ideas.

In crafting an innovation-driven governance and leadership model with a view toward establishing and maintaining a culture of innovation, here are some key strategic questions to consider:

* How would our leadership/governance/organizational chart look different if we were to *redraw* it around a culture of innovation?

* How would compensation systems and rewards and incentives for our teams look different if we were to *restructure* and *renegotiate* them around a culture of innovation?

* How would our external relationships (board of advisers, professional consultants, strategic partners) look different if we were to *reselect, re-engage,* and *redirect* them around an innovation-driven mission, values, and key objectives?

* How do we create more innovation pioneers, champions, influencers, mentors, coaches, and thought leaders within our organization so that innovation is long term and sustainable and *not* a fad or trend? How do we *reconnect* with our people and make this a priority? Can we truly change or influence an otherwise broken or underperforming structure, culture, system, or paradigm?

* How do we put less emphasis on the "rock stars" and give more recognition to the "roadies" who make it all happen? Many companies embody innovation in a particular person when it really takes a diverse team of tinkerers, testers, debuggers, fixers, troubleshooters, and maintenance groups to

drive long-term and sustainable innovation—but do we adequately reward their efforts and contributions to the overall process?

Leadership Archetypes in Fostering a Culture of Innovation

There is no single "right model" or "one size fits all" approach to leadership approaches or styles that will foster and support innovation. Imitating the best practices of another company that has little or nothing in common with your own will not move the needle of progress very far. Each board and leadership team must develop a culture system, budget, and process for fostering innovation that best fits the company's strengths and weaknesses, opportunities and limitations, budgetary constraints, history, marketplace, and skill sets.

Another critical factor is *consistency* and *continuity* of leadership and culture. It is virtually impossible for employees to innovate in a manner aligned with the leadership of the company's top priorities if there is a changing of the guard too often and projects die an early death because of a shift in the strategic agenda. At the peak of the recession in 2008, the average tenure of a CEO was less than 24 months, not nearly enough time for innovation to survive incubation for most types of projects.

In a study published in May 2007 by IBM Global Services, Innosight, and APQC, four major leadership archetypes were identified. Some companies fell comfortably into one type, while others used hybrids to foster innovation. The four archetypes are summarized in the table on the next page.

Sometimes a few simple but consistently and persistently

Internal Marketplace of Ideas (Google®, 3M)

* Employees are charged with creating new ideas, shaping them around internally to lobby for support, and implementing them to test feasibility and market acceptance.

Visionary Leader (Apple®, Facebook)

* A highly visible and visionary leader—such as Steve Jobs or Mark Zuckerberg—understands the future even better than his customers and motivates employees to zealously pursue that vision, and this process typically generates ideas that are unexpected and profound.

Innovation Via Rigor (P&G, Samsung)

* Companies develop systems, processes, budgeting approvals, and similar systems to produce innovative results, multiple global R&D, and customer research centers, tools, and studies that are used to gather and analyze data for new products and services.

Collaboration-Driven Innovation (Vodaphone, Mayo Clinic)

* Companies rely on external alliances and partnerships to drive the innovation process. Early-stage partnerships are frequent and abundant until traction is gained and early success is documented, thereby leading to more formal joint ventures or even acquisitions.

applied rules can facilitate a culture of innovation. Here are a few to consider:

* **Google's 70/20/10 rule:** Each employee should spend 70 percent of her time working on the core business, 20 percent working on ways to extend or expand the core, and 10 percent thinking completely outside the box. The 20 percent window has been very productive and accounts for the creation and launch of many of Google's newer services, including Gmail, Google News, Orbit, and AdServe. In fact, nearly half of Google's entire

new product launches were birthed during the 20 percent open creativity window.

* **3M's 30 percent/4 rule:** At 3M, 30 percent of total sales must result from products introduced within the past four years, forcing innovative products to have an almost immediate impact on the top and bottom lines. This rule is supported by the 15 percent rule, which allows technical personnel to spend 15 percent of their time on projects of their own choosing without any prior approvals.

* **UPM mandatory sabbaticals:** UPM, a Finnish paper manufacturer, requires its engineers to have mandatory on-site sabbaticals with value-chain players such as paper manufacturing machine makers and large commercial printers in order to ensure that R&D teams stay close to the needs of the customer.

* **Where-the-rubber-meets-the-road rule:** Rubbermaid introduces 365 new products a year and improves 5,000 of its existing products each year, as well. It enters a new-product category every 12 to 18 months and, like 3M, its goal is to obtain one-third of its sales from products introduced within the past five years.

* **IBM Fellows Program:** IBM fosters innovation and intrapreneurship (discussed in Chapter 3) by rewarding engineers who have worked for the company for 15 to 20 years and who have demonstrated a proclivity for creativity and productivity with a 5-year package of benefits and executive-level salary and access to resources to work on a self-selected and self-directed innovation project.

A commitment to being a bona fide intellectual capital agrarian as a company requires a full or partial abandonment of traditional or historical approaches to product development or growth. What works in the old-line core business divisions will not work when fostering new internal ventures. *The rules of the game must change and be supported and reinforced at the top echelons of the organization.* The new rules are as follows:

* There must be tolerance for higher levels of failure or loss than are typically tolerated in current core business lines.

* There must be willingness to embrace greater uncertainty and a foggier outlook through the corporate windshield.

* There must be an ability to withstand more inconsistent and lumpier revenue streams and profit hopes.

* There must be a restraint on micromanagement or short-term thinking with respect to the venturing projects.

* There must be a commitment to a more autonomous management structure.

* There must be a *real* commitment of financial and nonfinancial resources (within target project budgets and performance milestones.

* There must be genuine and holistic diversity in building the teams that will implement the venturing project, but not in a way that derails a shared vision or the ability to make decisions.

* There must be complete "buy-in"; nobody should serve on innovation or creativity teams who does not want to be there.

* There must be balance in the size and scope of the teams; they must be small enough to get things done and communicate frequently and large enough to ensure a steady influx of new ideas.

In sum, the leadership of the company must be willing to mimic the dynamics of the prototypical relationship between a venture capitalist and an entrepreneur—committing resources subject to certain controls but, at the core, giving the team enough rope to either build a viable company or hang themselves.

Building Agrarian Teams

Great teams drive innovation to higher and more productive and profitable levels. Intellectual capital agrarian teams have clear goals for the outputs of their creative energy, clear objectives of research and development, and clear roles and responsibilities to prevent overlap, waste, inefficiency, or turf wars. Teams are guided by trust, rapport, and esprit de corps among members and a commitment to organizational values that transcend any individual agendas or aspirations. These teams share a common purpose, a common reward, and a deep commitment to driving shareholder value as a direct and indirect result of their efforts. Communication among team members is thoughtful, respectful, honest, candid, and compassionate and is aimed at both accountability and performance. Teams are diverse in a number of ways, from gender/race/age/religion to personality types and core strengths. As shown in Figure 2-1, an intellectual capital agrarian team typically has at least four key operational members, each contributing in a critical way.

There are typically four separate humans performing these various roles. Rarely will you find the characteristics needed to perform these roles all in one person or even two people. Each must be authorized and empowered and have access to the resources she needs to perform her roles and accomplish her mission-critical tasks. And these teams may be focused on the development of one or more critical technologies or developments but are typically more effective when working on a narrower set of initiatives rather than on a set of diluted innovation objectives.

Figure 2-1. The essential functions of the intellectual capital agrarian team.

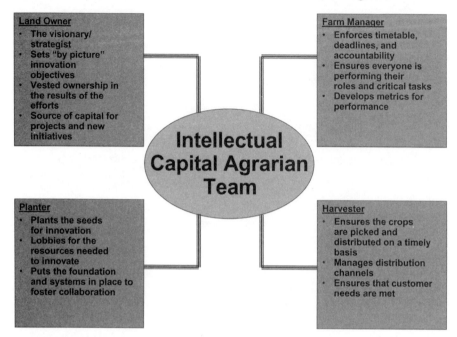

A Culture of Innovation: An Organizational Self-Assessment

The Ten A's

* **Attitude:** What are the *leader* and the *organization's* views on *innovation* and *creativity?* Is there a genuine willingness to take (and reward) risk?

* **Appetite:** Does the management have the necessary fire in the belly? How *hungry* is this company to be a market and technological leader?

* **Aptitude:** Are we *capable* of innovating? Have we put systems and creative processes in place? What strategic relationships do we need to put in place? Do we have the right partners and advisers?

* **Alignment:** How can we retool the organizational chart to get the "Right People on the Right Bus" with a shared and consistent vision and a track record and commitment to innovation?

* **Access:** Is there access to the human and financial resources needed to innovate?

* **Allocation:** Are we allocating the time and resources necessary to successfully innovate, create, and harvest intangible assets?

* **Accountability:** Who will be responsible for managing and measuring the results intended to favor this process?

* **Ascension:** Are we (*really*) ready to take things to the next level?

* **Attribution:** Are we building on a secure foundation (or are there cracks that should be sealed or additional blocks that need to be put in place)?

* **Adaptability:** Are we (*really*) ready to *change* the risk/reward ratio within our:

  + Culture (and comfort zone)?
  + Compensation systems?
  + Returns to shareholders?
  + Relationships with partners, vendors, and customers?
  + Internal roles and responsibilities (including controls, leadership, and cross-border/cross-cultural relationships)?

Best Practices in Fostering and Maintaining a Culture of Innovation

Over the years, I have developed and observed a wide variety of best practices for fostering and establishing on a sustainable basis a genuine culture of innovation. These must be embraced at all levels of the organization to be effective. They include:

* **Innovation, like the spreading of fertilizer, is messy, lumpy, smelly, expensive, and unpredictable.** Innovation rarely happens in a neat and sequential fashion. Imposing too many rules or protocols will retard or overly restrict the process. And there must be a commitment to spread the fertilizer frequently, consistently, and across the entire field, not just once in a while to "pet" projects. And the results are not always what you would predict or expect. An often-cited example is Proctor & Gamble's Olestra, which was accidentally discovered by company researchers in 1968 while researching fats that could be easily digested by infants. The proprietary ingredient evolved as a key feature of potato chips and snack foods in the mid-1990s, but sales began dropping when many consumers were not willing to experience abdominal cramping and loose stools in exchange for reduced fat and calories. Facing falling sales in the United States and complete bans on Olestra as a food additive in the United Kingdom, Canada, and many other countries, P&G began exploring other applications for their proprietary compound. In recent years, the chemistry behind Olestra has been used in environmental remediation, industrial lubricants, and paint additives; as a base for deck stains; and as a lubricant for small power tools. If you create processes that are appropriate for the levels of innovation and creativity goals that have been set, you create an environment that supports this process. If you are overly process oriented, budget driven, or linear in your thinking, you may be putting too many walls around a process that needs room to breathe.

* **Embrace the headless tiger.** In January 2011, Steve Jobs announced that he would be taking a second extended medical leave of absence from Apple, and the company's stock price promptly fell by more than $20, even though the company's lead-

ership would be put into the capable hands of Timothy Cook, the chief operating officer (COO) since 1998. Many great companies accomplish innovation objectives under the leadership of household-name visionary leaders such as Bill Gates and Andy Grove. But we all know that people don't stay with companies forever, and the culture must be prepared to innovate with or without their day-to-day presence. Companies that are overly dependent on the physical presence of their founders cannot be sustained. Team-driven innovation will create leaders at all levels that can sustain, perpetuate, and strengthen the founder's vision long after he or she steps down from the helm of the company. Investments in training, commitments to empowerment and delegation, and the development of meaningful succession plans are all critical elements of this process.

* **The only thing that is certain is change.** In our volatile economy and fast-paced, technology-driven world, the unknown has become the only real thing we can count on as known. As soon as we become comfortable with something, we can be assured that something new will replace it sooner rather than later. New versions, new editions, new models, new flavors, new packaging, new styles, new pricing models, and new distribution channels are coming out so fast that many of us are afraid that our newest gadget will become obsolete before we even leave the mall.

* **Leave the safety of the cave.** Our primal ancestors understood that there were real predators waiting for them outside the safety of their caves. Many of us still live our lives the same way; we always want to know what is around the corner, what comes next. Life is not as sequential and as predictable as we would like it to be, and this is certainly the case with innovation and creativity. New missions and new goals bring out that hard-wired DNA memory of the initial fear of the unknown.

 * **Avoid cynics and naysayers.** There is a major difference between cynics and skeptics, between Doubting Dora and Debbie Downer. Dora, the skeptic, is a healthy contributor to the innovation process because she asks all the right questions, even if they are with a negative bias. Debbie Downer is driven by her own insecurities and will find something wrong with anything and everything. Creativity needs both a yin and a yang to make a perfect circle, but it does not need anyone throwing cold water on the process just to protect her seat in the sun.

 * **Blaze new trails.** Ralph Waldo Emerson wrote, "Do not go where the path may lead, instead go where there is no path at all and leave a trail." Emerson understood the core precepts of innovation. It is not just the willingness to travel where no one has gone before; it is the value added by creating a new trail that others can follow. Trailblazing is not just about the process of discovery; it is about the outputs of invention. Edison was guided by this principle in all of his toils in the laboratory and his bold willingness to defy convention in order to accomplish invention.

 * **Trust in yourself and your coworkers.** People don't innovate without self-confidence, and teams can't perform without trust. Trust in your ability to make a significant contribution in your own way to your organization, and trust in your team and the system to respect and embrace your contributions. Trust must exist at the peer-to-peer level, at the cross-departmental level, and at the supervisor-subordinate level. Nothing is more inspiring than praise that is earned and the feeling that those who evaluate your performance believe deeply in the quality and integrity of your work. Trust is a type of fuel and an empowering

and liberating energy force that inspires creativity and innovation.

* **Empower people to let down their guards.** Nobody can innovate while putting out fires or living in the present tense. Innovation by its very nature requires conditions where team members can clear away enough of the muck on their daily windshields to peer forward into the future to sense and explore new possibilities and envision new realities. There must be a "safe" environment where the outputs of the visioning can be exposed, explored, and discussed without ridicule or too much negativity. Once the idea has been massaged, shaped, and restated, the more burdensome tasks of execution, adoption, and sustainability begin. Participants in the process must understand the critical differences between simple ideation or invention *and* the more complex tasks of sustainable innovation and value creation, but you can't have one without the other.

* **Who let the RATS out?** An effective and sustainable innovation process requires a systematic approach and commitment to the deployment of Resources, Advocacy, Testing, and Sustainable (RATS) demand. Resources include human capital, time, equipment supplies, and the environmental capital to bring the idea to fruition. Advocacy requires internal and external supporters who will help attract resources and emotional support for the project. Testing and evaluation requires an environment that allows the idea to be shaped, refined, remolded, and eventually placed into some quantifiable model that predicts financial return on time and capital invested. Sustainable demand requires the identification of target customers, markets, channels, and potential strategic partners that demonstrate the size and scope of the potential buyers of the product or source, as well as the partners needed to reach these customers.

* **Hey, who interrupted my disruption?** Sometimes creativity and innovation can grow within the four walls of an organization over a long period of time on a gradual basis. But, in most cases, they need to be jump-started by an executive at a high level who is not afraid to disrupt or creatively destroy the culture and the status quo. The change can be radical or transformational or just a reset and reboot of top priorities and budget allocations and reward systems. But, like all momentum, pauses, fits, and starts or any other interruption to the disruption can derail the disruption, and, with CEOs and leaders playing musical chairs on what seems like a constant basis, it has been challenging for those responsible for innovation to determine a clear direction or gain any real innovation momentum.

* **Listen to the customer and the marketplace—carefully but not literally.** Customers and markets are not shy, especially in a Web 2.0–driven interconnected world, about giving you feedback about the types of breakthroughs and incremental innovation they want to experience in order to become or stay your customer. But listen with a careful ear, and do not take everything they say literally; read between the lines. Henry Ford is often credited with saying that, had he asked the consumer what he really wanted in the early 1900s, the customer would have said, "Faster and stronger horses."

* **World Series are won with singles and doubles.** Baseball historians will explain that, as exciting as home runs may be to watch from the fans' seats, most batting titles, RBI leaders, and World Series team winners are determined by the nine men who can consistently hit singles and doubles, especially at clutch points in the game when runners are in scoring positions. The same holds true for innovation. Many CEOs swing

for the fences with the hopes of breakthrough innovation, but most innovative growth companies succeed through lots of smaller projects and incremental innovations. CEOs must be careful not to demonstrate or marginalize those who are working on hitting singles and doubles; that will only frustrate the process and virtually ensure that no games are won.

  * **Cast your net widely in your quest for new ideas.** Innovation and creativity can come from many sources—both inside and outside the organization. Look to customers, vendors, channel partners, and even competitors as sources for new ideas and guidance about areas where products and services can be improved or strengthened. Do not be passive or protective of the process—and do not become defensive when suggestions cut deep into the heart of the organization. Candor can be painful, but without pain there is no gain. Do not allow your culture to suffer from NIH ("not invented here") syndrome, which assumes that ideas not generated by the leaders of the organization cannot possibly be worthy of consideration.

  * **Don't be bored by boards.** Related to the preceding best practice is the establishment and management of dynamic advisory boards, scientific or technical development boards, customer or channel partner input boards, and so on—all designed to be different types of sounding boards for new ideas and problem solving. These are *not* formal boards of directors and will need to be provided with a clear charter, mission, and reward system. Choose board members carefully, and be sensitive to diversity and relevance in determining their overall composition. Look at board dynamics, participation, and collaboration to make them effective, and put systems in place to avoid grandstanding, conflicts of interest, or apathy.

* **Harvest the power of your networks.** When I graduated from law school in 1986, I had "eight scraps" of paper with landline phone numbers written in pencil of people who might help me pursue a successful career. My network was dormant, nonconnected, and incapable of updating itself if these contacts changed jobs or responsibilities. Today's college or professional school graduate is likely to enter the workforce with thousands of electronic contacts via social networks such as LinkedIn, Facebook, and Plaxo. These networks are dynamic, interconnected, and constantly evolving. The connectivity of our society is driving productivity, innovation, creativity, and the forging of strategic relationships in a manner we could have only imagined a short 25 years ago.

* **Make it fun—and remain open minded.** Marcus Buckingham, in his book *Put Your Strengths to Work*, observes that nearly four-fifths of the working population hate or strongly dislike their jobs. Innovation requires passion, and passion can't be faked or contrived; it must be real and genuine for the seeds of creativity to truly grow into harvestable crops. Fun empowers creativity and allows people to see things they could not or would not see otherwise. Fun is (and can be) functional and productive. Game playing, experimenting, role playing, team-building exercises, informal gatherings, retreats, and parties can *all* facilitate creative thinking and an innovative culture. They liberate the brain to think more clearly and break down barriers and walls that are impediments to innovation. It is also critical to always be open minded—what was initially intended may not be the function that has the greatest upside. The bio/pharma industry embraces this notion, and it has rewarded certain companies handsomely. For example, in 1988, Allergan acquired the rights to Botox as a remedy for uncontrollable blinking. But, over time,

out-of-the-box thinking allowed executives to understand its capability as an antiwrinkle treatment, and, after the company won FDA approval, in 2002, the rest is history. When Viagra was first being tested by Pfizer in the early 1990s, it was intended as a cure for certain cardiovascular diseases, and one of the observed side effects of the compound was a sustained erection. Needless to say, a little repackaging and repositioning, and the rest is again history.

There is a story of an old man who was planting tree saplings on the side of the road when some hecklers came upon him and began ridiculing his efforts. One said, "You old fool, why do you toil in the hot sun to plant trees whose fruits you will never enjoy?" To which he responded, "We plant trees so that the next generation will be able to eat, as my forefathers did for me." Building a culture of innovation, productivity, and creativity is a long-term and multigenerational process. Patience must triumph over short-term greed and the pressure for immediate results. As we examine in Chapter 3, a culture of innovation must be rooted in a commitment to intrapreneurship, where people feel motivated, appreciated, and rewarded for their efforts, their contributions, their sacrifice, and their commitment to the well-being and best interests of the organization.

As Sam Walton insightfully observed in building Wal-Mart: *"Appreciate everything your associates do for the business. A paycheck is one thing; how much we are appreciated is something else. Nothing else can quite substitute for a few well-chosen, well-timed, sincere words of praise. They're absolutely fee and worth a fortune."*

CHAPTER 3

Irrigating the Field: Embracing Intrapreneurship

Today more than ever, we must cultivate the creative and innovative potential of every employee in the organization. Everyone in the organization must be capable of thinking creatively and be willing to try new approaches which transcend their own roles, departments, and processes.

—ANDREW PAPAGEORGE, CHIEF INNOVATION
STRATEGIST AT GOINNOVATE!

As discussed in Chapter 2, the leadership of the company or organization must be committed to establishing, maintaining, and supporting (with resources, both tangible and intangible) a genuine culture committed to all types of innovation. Once this culture has been put firmly in place and the seeds of innovation have been planted, the irrigation process begins with a parallel commitment to building an organizational foundation built on pillars of *intrapreneurship.*

As farmers know, irrigation is both an art and a science. Apply too little water at the wrong time and to the wrong places, and crops will die of drought. Apply too much water, and crops will die of flood. Corporate leaders must find the same delicate balance in creating systems and rewards to foster intrapreneurship and to uncover hidden opportunities. If incentives and resources are too sparse, employees and teams will be slow to respond, and an innovation drought will set in. If too many resources are applied all at once, there may be confusion of strategic priorities or too much encouragement to walk out the door with new technology in hand. Using the right tools to irrigate intrapreneurship is also critical. Many CEOs wind up using a fire hose when they should be using a garden hose or sprinkler system; this may concentrate too much water in one place at one time or leaving other projects to die of thirst, thereby destroying the project or putting out the creative fires. In other cases, the CEO may be spending too much time putting out fires, thereby wasting precious time and water that could be better utilized irrigating new ideas and growing fresh talent. It is also critical to understand that irrigation systems are designed to be the strategic and controllable offset to one key variable that you cannot control—Mother Nature; the level at which you must irrigate your crops will be driven in part by how much rain actually falls in any given season. Market and economic conditions in business function the same way as Mother Nature does—it is impossible for company leaders to control them, so they need to monitor them carefully to determine how many or how few additional nutrients will be required to facilitate the company's growth and the creation of additional intellectual assets.

Intrapreneurship has been defined in many ways, but for the purposes of this book, we will define it this way: a person or team within a large corporation that takes direct responsibility for turning an idea into a profitable finished product through assertive risk taking, the gathering of internal resources, and support and innovation. It is *not* merely invention, which may create something new but which typically does not by itself create value to customers or drive shareholder value.

When intrapreneurship is applied inside the four walls of a growing company committed to a culture of innovation, great things begin to happen. People feel empowered, directed, rewarded, appreciated, invigorated, and reconnected to the reasons they chose *this* career path and this company as a place to spend 10 to 12 hours a day. They feel like they are part of something much larger than themselves and realize that their rewards for work far transcend their individual corporation as they become true drivers and contributors to the maximization of shareholder value. These happier and more challenged employees are not only considerably more productive; they are also more loyal and tend to stay at the company much longer, significantly reducing costly employee turnover expenses.

Examples of Crops Yielded by Intrapreneurship		
Mothership	**Intrapreneurial Project Supported**	**Crops Yielded**
Microsoft	Entry into the consumer gaming market	Xbox
Sony	Recovery from the Walkman meltdown and	

(continues)

	locating an electronic pairing for its excellent television line	PlayStation
Kodak	Transforming the company as the photo paper business dies and is replaced by digital media	Kodak printers, cameras, digital media management and software.
Cisco	Transcending its back-office router reputation and being out front and branded in bringing people together	The Cisco Human Network and line of products/systems
Procter & Gamble	Developing innovative strategies for age-old problems	Swiffer line of products

Intrapreneurship and Leadership

The board of directors and executive team must set the tone and initially write the playbook for the parameters of intrapreneurship within the company. The playbook details the rules for success and failure, resource allocation, ownership of inventions, rewards and incentives, and strategies and structures for intrapreneurship. Innovation and intrapreneurship can be a central part of the company's mission, values, and branding, as is the case with Southwest Airlines, Walt Disney Company, and DuPont, or assume a much lower priority in the strategic food chain. If there is too wide a gap or disconnect between a company's intrapreneurial playbook and the skill sets and desires of the employees who are supposed to be acting as entrepreneurs, all innovation efforts will derail. Visionary boards and CEOs surrounded by traditional-thinking corporate managers will make innovation virtually impossible; it's like trying to drive a sports car on a racetrack without an engine. Conversely, creative and forward-thinking employees whose projects are constantly being shut down or mired in red tape will either leave or, worse, just give up and fall back into their risk-free daily patterns. Alignment and shared values are critical, and all employees should have a crystal-clear picture as to *how* and *where* they fit into the intrapreneurship process and *why* it is mission-critical to the organization and the stakeholders.

The bridge, the glue, and the catalyst responsible for this alignment is typically the chief innovation officer ("CIO"). This is a relatively new position in global companies, and the precise job description is still evolving as of this writing. Companies as diverse as Coca-Cola, Humana, Owens Corning, AMD, and Citigroup all include the CIO among their top leadership positions as the pressure to innovate and harvest intellectual capital rises to the top of corporate agendas. But only a handful of companies have made this commitment, and there are tens of thousands of organizations that have no senior person or team accountable for managing innovation and fostering intrapreneurship.

Some common themes have emerged in building the position descriptions for the CIO:

* **Setting a common and consistent set of innovation values and policies.** The CIO needs to develop companywide values and policies so that everyone is singing from the same hymnal and must communicate these policies through training and by sharing success stories and best practices.

* **Determining intrapreneurship strategies and structures.** Intrapreneurship can take many forms, as demonstrated

in Figure 3-1. Larger traditional companies tend to gather everything and everyone together under an R&D department that may service multiple divisions within the conglomerate. But more nimble and progressive companies are turning to ad hoc venture teams, new venture divisions and groups, innovation centers, internal VC funds and research growth, offsite "skunkworks" operations, and even innovation sabbaticals to foster intrapreneurship. External strategies include outsourcing, university research projects teaming and partnering, cross-licensing, and M&A and joint ventures to achieve intrapreneurship objectives.

＊ **Attracting and retaining intrapreneurial talent.** The CIO must work closely with the human resources department to ensure that innovative workers are recruited, rewarded, and retained. Policies must be put in place to both recognize the accomplishments and the failures/efforts of creative teams financially and nonfinancially. The company must be flexible

Figure 3-1. The new agrarian strategic flow chart.

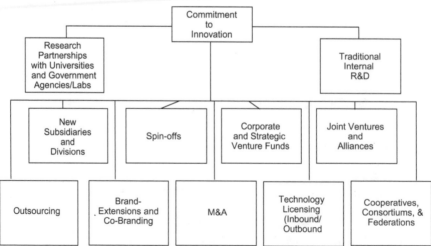

enough to reward people who help drive genuine shareholder value and keep them *connected* to the energy level and culture that attracted them to the company in the first place. This is not as easy as it seems, even with the most high-profile, rapid-growth companies. Early employees of Facebook have already begun leaving to start their own companies as the excitement of a start-up morphs into the potential doldrums of a larger, more established environment. Google has also struggled recently to hold some of its most creative people as the attractiveness of smaller, high-growth companies such as LinkedIn, Zynga, Twitter, Asana, and Jumo offer an ability to replicate the innovation birthing process. The CIO must ensure that the best and the brightest stay loyal and stay put or at least know how and where to find replacements for them if they depart for greener pastures.

* **Executing high-level innovation priorities and evaluating bottom-up proposals.** Innovation and intrapreneurship are *both* top-down and bottom-up when the systems are working properly. The CIO must develop the screens and filters for evaluating ideas; assigning resources, teams, and capital to them; and making sure that organizationwide innovative goals are met. Greenhouses and safe places must be established where new ideas have a chance to be vetted and prototypes and working models/proofs of concept tests can be piloted. The selection and management of test markets, early customer adopters, advocacy groups, market influencers, and early-stage channel partners are all within the CIO's domain. The knowledge and the best practices that are gathered when these assumptions are tested must be shared across company lines and, where and when appropriate, with external partners and stakeholders.

* **Collaborating and managing innovation.** As we explore in Chapter 4, the CIO must develop, implement, main-

tain, and improve the company's intellectual asset management (IAM) programs, policies, and systems to facilitate collaboration and cooperation with all internal and external stakeholders and foster harvesting strategies to unlock and drive shareholder value.

* **Serving as the chief steward for the company's brands and trade dress.** The CIO must work closely with the company's marketing, branding, and sales executives to protect and enhance the company's brands, slogans, designs, reputation, and Web 2.0 campaigns and communities. As discussed in Chapter 8, these intangible assets are increasing in strategic importance every day as a source of potential revenues and profits. And, from a budget management perspective, the beauty lies in the fact that they often already exist, but an effort must be made to uncover them enough to begin the extraction of shareholder value.

* **Serving as the gatekeeper and taxi dispatcher for companywide innovation initiatives.** In a company dedicated to intrapreneurship, somebody needs to be responsible for "herding the cats" and for ensuring that the trains are all running on time. The CIO is the train conductor and the taxi dispatcher who helps ensure that intrapreneurial projects are coming in on time and on budget. He or she must be in the loop and have a full understanding of the variables that will influence costs; the timetable; and the metrics that will be used for determining success and failure and target returns on investment.

* **Serving as liaison to outside advisers and stakeholders (e.g., lawyers, technical support, co-investors, partners).** Working together with more traditional role players, such as the CFO and the general counsel, the CIO must be a critical point of contact with the outside advisers, consultants, partners,

and investors who influence innovation results. He or she is the "face" of innovation progress to the outside world.

The Strategic Core of Intrapreneurship

Variables That Support Intrapreneurship

*   An executive vision that is shared and accepted by all employees
*   An understanding of the market/industry by the employees involved
*   Small, flat organizations, at least within the area where intrapreneurship is happening
*   Teamwork
*   Freedom and encouragement to develop ideas
*   Absence of fear of failing, of retribution, or of ridicule when an idea fails because of external factors

Who is responsible for fostering the intrapreneurial culture in an organization? Not the President or the CEO, but *everyone*. The innovative spirit must be felt from the bottom to the top. Companies must create a climate in which *anyone* can decide to innovate.

How to Foster Intrapreneurship

*   **Listen.** Company leadership must be willing to recognize good ideas from any part of the organization.
*   **Cut the red tape.** An efficient business approval process is necessary. Often, a flat corporate hierarchy is more efficient at getting ideas approved.
*   **Don't be afraid to fail.** With risk comes reward. Good ideas will never be voiced if failing comes at a high price. But people also need to realize responsibility.

(continues)

* **Share the credit.** Leaders who take all the credit for ideas will find few followers. Ideas won't be forthcoming if there is no reward. Be comfortable with ambiguity.

* **Break the mold.** The greatest innovations are always utterly alien at first. Don't be afraid to strike out in a new direction.

Cultures of Intrapreneurship and Innovation

* Create cross-functional teams, and collaborate (with a "seat at the table" for younger and lower-level team members if the younger people have fresh ideas and lower-level members avoid disruptive ideas.

* Have a healthy impatience.

* Seed grants for "umbilical cord" projects.

* Seek consistency across divisions that foster and support/ reward creativity.

* Install high-profile negotiation/reward systems that embrace results.

* Have face time in the trenches, with your ears close to the ground and your eyes wide open.

Companies committed to intrapreneurship are run like King Arthur ran the Knights of the Roundtable—as long as each knight was productive, he was left alone to manage (and live or die in part) by the success of his own fiefdom. Common core values, systems, and disciplines across the board are shared, but each division has its own profit-and-loss (P&L) responsibilities and its own resources and partners for bringing products and services to the marketplace. These companies create systems where smaller teams and resources compete for funding and resources from the mothership in many of the same ways entrepreneurs must compete for resources in the capital markets.

Companies that support intrapreneurship as an implementing tool for achieving innovation and an irrigation method for growing strong inventories of intellectual capital view employees as resources, not expenses. Teams are assembled for the purposes of creating, not for maintaining. People are rewarded for breaking the status quo, not for protecting it. Some degree of failure is a given and is embraced as long as it provides a learning experience. Micromanagement is tossed out the window in favor of a hands-off, more creative culture that seeks to mimic the experiences of smaller company entrepreneurs all operating within the larger mothership.

The rewards for creating new products and services can include significant bonuses, equity awards, internal and external recognition, and even spin-offs into newly created, partially owned subsidiaries in lieu of an MBO or a divestiture. These spin-offs can drive shareholder value at both the parent and subsidiary level. We take a look at spin-offs in more detail in the next section.

Spin-Offs

Spin-offs have been characterized as a strategy different from M&A, but breaking up a company can be an effective means to profit and growth. Smaller, more independent subsidiaries lead to a more focused strategy and managerial autonomy that allows for greater responsibility and increased incentive for creativity and productivity.

Studies show that spin-offs during the 1990s have beaten the market by about 10 percentage points annually. The reasons cited include the increased stake executives have in the new venture, their extreme commitment to success, and increased time and resources invested in the project that would not have been provided by the parent company.

* Spin-offs of divisions, product groups, or teams of innovators can create a new entity with the ability to leverage noncore business lines into additional revenue for the parent company and reinforce to those left behind that innovation and intrapreneurship can pay off for them, as well.

* Spin-offs can streamline parent company operations while still fostering innovation and intrapreneurship.

* Spin-offs can protect the brand from noncore-business dilution and loss of focus.

* Spin-offs can offer an outlet for creativity as well as an opportunity to increase revenues and, perhaps, share prices for both companies.

As shown in Figure 3-2, the spin-off process consists of three phases:

1. *The decision phase:* Includes all factors leading to the decision to spin off.
2. *The separation phase:* Comprises the strategic and organizational separation of the two companies.

Figure 3-2. Key components of the spin-off process.

The Spin-off Process

	PARENT COMPANY		
DECISION	Intrapreneurs & Leading Innovators	and/or	Business Units & Subsidiaries	**PHASE 1**

Idea generation and innovative development leads to spin-off decision by parent company

SEPARATION — **PHASE 2**

| **POST-SEPARATION** | Parent Company | New Enterprise | **RELATIONSHI** **PHASE 3** |

3. *The post-separation phase:* Begins with the independent operation of parent and spin-off and ends when no more preferential agreements or relations between parent and spin-off exist.

Spin-offs are an effective way to harvest and harness innovation by unlocking and liberating a key intangible asset or project as its own entity, with its own governance, budgets, and decision-making process, and removing the handcuffs created by the red tape of a large organization. Multiple studies and best practices have confirmed that there is a strong correlation between a management style that allows for independence in employees' decision making and employees' performance and creativity.

A prime example of this model of governance is Thermo Electron. The company rewards risk takers and innovators by creating opportunities to pursue spin-offs via research projects that have profit-making potential. Those projects that are commercially viable are often made into subsidiary companies and spun off to the public. Thermo Electron had nine successful spin-offs in the 1980s. The new entities were often managed by the engineers and scientists who had spearheaded the research. This managerial style provided an incentive for innovation by creating job advancement opportunities for the creative employees. Spinning off companies has also allowed the company to give managers stock options in their businesses to further stimulate their creativity. Thus, it was able to recruit and retain talented executives who preferred to run their own show. Thermo Electron's successful spin-off strategy has earned it the labels "venture capital holding company," "research and development firm," and "a perpetual idea machine."

Pervasive Software, a spin-off from Novell, Inc., split from its parent because it felt its potential was being overlooked. As a separate entity, Pervasive is run more like a start-up. It has a smaller staff, a smaller budget, and rapid growth and enjoys increasing customer demand. The spin-off allowed management to give more freedom and ownership of the project to its employees. Opportunities were created for the staff to "pour their hearts and souls into a project" and to see themselves more as entrepreneurs and less as division employees. While the spin-off put more responsibility on the individual employees' shoulders, the new governance structure resulted in increased productivity and innovation and larger profit margins.

Another example is VM Ware, which was spun out of the data-storage conglomerate EMC in 2008 in order to unlock more of the subsidiary's value for EMC shareholders and to help the division attract and retain talent in the rapidly growing virtualization software industry. When EMC acquired VM Ware in 2004, it had 300 employees; by 2007, the team had reached 3,000. As of late 2010, the share price of VM Ware (VMH) was at $89 per share with a standalone market capitalization of $9.9 billion and a total team of more than 7,000 employees.

As yet a third example, McDonald's Corporation bought 92 percent of Denver-based Chipotle Mexican Grille in 1999 and spun it off as a separate company in early 2006. At the time of the spin-off, Chipotle operated 450 restaurants nationwide. As of December 2010, its stock traded at an impressive $238 per share, and the company had a market capitalization of $7.4 billion, 23,000 employees, and 956 restaurants in the United States and Canada.

As companies are under increased pressure to unlock shareholder value and drive innovation, the trend toward spin-offs is likely to continue well into the 2010s. And it is not limited to larger companies. Small and mid-size companies, universities, government agencies, and trade associations are all working with spin-off and restructuring strategies to foster stronger intrapreneurship and opportunity. Nonprofit organizations like the American Association of Airport Executives (AAAE), in Alexandria, Virginia, have spun off technology assets into for-profit affiliates to harvest opportunity and to attract third-party investors.

Many large global companies have enjoyed tremendous success by adapting the principles of intrapreneurship within a culture of innovation. Irrigation efforts have sprung many tall beanstalks within the walls of Deere, 3M, IBM, Hewlett-Packard, Xerox, and Procter & Gamble. Some companies have gotten so good at intrapreneurship that they have taken on the role as consultants to others. For example, 3M has been acquiring additional R&D companies and facilities as its "client base" of external innovation clients continues to grow—and as others realize that, if R&D is not a core strength, it may be more effective to outsource the process to the experts with a proven track record of innovation.

3M's Seven Pillars of Intrapreneurship

Although 3M is more than 100 years old, it is still a leader in cutting-edge innovation. Its "Seven Pillars of Innovation" are a big reason why it is still a pioneer and thought leader in innovation. Here are 3-M's seven core principles.

1. A company must be committed to innovation. 3M has proven this through its commitment to R&D investment, spending more than $1.5 billion of its 2008 revenues on R&D, an unusually high ratio of nearly 8 percent measured against its total revenue of $24 billion that same year.

(continues)

2. A corporate culture of innovation must be stringently maintained. Keep stories of past glories flowing, for example, how 3M invented the first audio tapes. Immerse new employees in this culture of performance and innovation.

3. A broad base of technology is crucial, as is leveraging past and current innovations in developing new and diverse technologies.

4. Networking, both internally and externally, is very important. Communication between divisional employees and outside innovators can break down silos and encourage opportunities for advice and team building.

5. Motivation and reward structures can play a major role in raising the bar for innovators. 3M sets individual expectations and rewards employees for exemplary performance. It has established a dual career ladder that allows veteran researchers to move up without becoming managers, and there is a formal recognition process for scientific achievers each year.

6. Quantifying efforts can help a company to recognize how much revenue is being generated from which products, assessing how well the company has distributed the R&D dollar.

7. Research must be market based. Rather than developing backwards with an "If you build it, they will come" mentality, companies need to innovate on the basis of needs in the marketplace. 3M did this research with their Post-it Photo Paper for printing digital images, which can be stuck anywhere a Post-it can.

Why Does Intrapreneurship Go Ignored or Misunderstood in So Many Companies?

In most companies, management and/or project team members focus on the "normal course of day-to-day business" without developing those ideas that can lead to improved profit or brand recognition. The most common barriers to intrapreneurship include:

* Lack of time (too busy)
* Lack of desire (too lazy)
* Lack of skills/expertise (too ignorant)
* Lack of vision (too focused on one's own niche)
* Lack of resources (too capital constrained)
* Lack of leadership (too thin at the top)
* Lack of market (too focused on technical excellence)

CHAPTER 4

Caring for the Fruits of the Harvest: Intellectual Asset Management (IAM)

Knowledge idle in a database is like food in a freezer. Nothing ever came out in better shape than it went in.

—FRANCES CAIRNCROSS, AUTHOR OF
THE COMPANY OF THE FUTURE

Ask any farmer managing his crops or any CEO making her widgets whether he or she has a system in place to manage inventories and the person will look at you as if you are insane. Of course, either will respond, "How could we not have systems, processes, and protocols in place to protect, manage, track, and distribute our tangible assets?" To not have systems in place would be gross mismanagement and a travesty with respect to a manager's fiduciary obligations to shareholders. So why then, in a society driven by knowledge, brands, know-how, and intangible assets, do we not have the same disciplines and duties in place regarding assets that we can't necessarily touch and feel but that are clearly driving the lion's share of the market value for Apple, Google, IBM, 3M, Amazon, Netflix, and Priceline? Why, at a time and place in our evolution when intangible assets are the key premiere drivers of revenue, opportunity, and profits, can leaders of companies not manage them like any other asset?

Cash is an asset, and we have CFOs, comptrollers, financial analysts, accountants, and clerks on hand to manage it. People are an asset, and we have chief administrative officers, HR managers, personnel specialists, and administrators to manage them. But, for the crops of knowledge, brands, systems, protocols, processes, know-how, show-how, channels, relationships, protocols, and best practices, we have no parallel positions on most organizational charts and no parallel systems to properly manage and extract value from these assets.

A few "enlightened" companies may have chief knowledge officers, but these are often glorified IT executives who apply principles of knowledge management (KM) to better manage and organize databases and perhaps gather internal best practices. Some truly progressive companies have chief innovation officers who are responsible for driving R&D and stimulating a creative culture, but these are often glorified HR executives or engineers who may understand either technology development *or* human performance and teamwork but rarely have cross-functional knowledge of both areas and who may be lacking experience in developing harvesting strategies. We build organizational charts and allocate resources to departments as if we were still doing business in 1975 instead of leaning into the future and building a team and a business model that is ready for 2015 and beyond.

When I speak at business conferences around the world to companies of all sizes and in all industries and ask them whether they have an intellectual asset management (IAM) system in place, I am typically greeted with blank stares. When a few feeble hands go up, I then ask whether their IAM systems have been effective and yielded profitable opportunities, and even fewer hands rise. When I ask whether their organizational chart has been retooled to reflect the transformational shift toward an intangible asset–driven economy, they look at me as if I just arrived from Mars. And, finally, when I ask them to name the person in the company who serves as the "CHIPPLE" (Chief Intellectual Property Protection and Leveraging Executive), they look at me as if I were from Venus. I am not aware of any extraterrestrial roots of my parents or grandparents, so I am pretty sure that I am not the one in the room at that point who is clueless and helpless. *How can we as leaders of companies and as fiduciary guardians of the entity's assets on behalf of our stakeholders continue to completely ignore the management and leveraging of our most important strategic assets?* How long will it take for lawsuits to be filed against the boards and leaders of companies for the "gross undermanagement and underleveraging" of the company's most important assets before we finally make this a top priority?

The time for companies of all sizes and in all industries around the globe to commit time and resources for the deployment of an effective multidisciplinary IAM system to properly cultivate, manage, and harvest intellectual assets, as set forth in Figure 4-1, is *now*. As stewards, guardians, and fiduciaries of the assets of the company, managers have a basic duty and obligation

Figure 4-1. The 12 critical success factors in IAM.

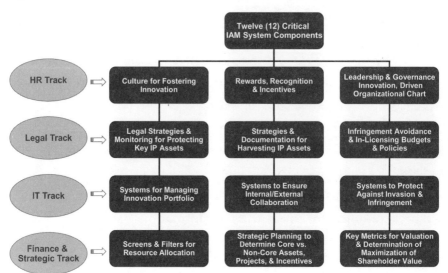

to maximize the value of these assets, especially in a post-Sarbanes-Oxley regulatory environment.

What Is Intellectual Asset Management?

Intellectual asset management (IAM) is a system for creating, organizing, prioritizing, and extracting value from a company's various sets of intellectual property assets. The intellectual capital and technical know-how of a company are among its most valuable assets, provide its greatest competitive advantages, and are the principal drivers of shareholder value, yet rarely do companies have adequate personnel, resources, and systems in place to properly manage and leverage these assets. IAM, as a matter of strategy and competitive intelligence gathering, also involves monitoring certain developments in the company's marketplace, such as:

* Gathering intelligence on direct, indirect, and potential competitors
* Monitoring developments abroad
* Keeping one step ahead of a constantly changing landscape (20,000 + new patents issued per month—and that is just in the United States)
* Maintaining license agreements and streams of royalty payments on both an inbound and outbound basis (e.g., royalty audits to ensure against underreporting [outbound] and overpayments [inbound]. Are you getting paid? Is there anyone you are paying that you shouldn't be paying? Are performance standards being met? Are you in relationships with the right parties? What could be done to strengthen existing relationships or distribution channels?

As the box on the next page illustrates, intellectual capital consists of many different types of human capital, intellectual property, and relationship capital. These are the key assets for driving growth and maximizing shareholder value in all types of economic conditions.

IAM also involves an understanding of how and where intellectual assets sit in the strategic parameters and food chain of the company. Three strategic views toward the use of intellectual capital have evolved in the boardroom over the past three decades.

1. **Traditional View.** IP assets enhance the company's competitive advantage and strengthen its ability to defend its competitive position in the marketplace; IP is seen as a barrier to entry and as a shield to protect market share (*reactive and passive approach*).

Types of Intangible Assets and Intellectual Property

Tangible assets

* Cash and credit lines
* Plant, inventory, and equipment
* Real estate
* IT and communications assets

Cultural assets

* Leadership and governance
* Organizational norms and habits
* Trust and integrity
* Mission, vision, and values
* Communication and goal setting
* Accountability
* Transparency
* Reward and compensation systems
* Decision-making systems

Relationship assets

* Corporate reputation and external/ internal brand image perception
* Status, strength value proposition, and influence over channel partner relationships (VARs, dealers, distributors, wholesalers, franchisees)
* Vendor relationships
* Customer relationships and loyalty to brands
* Investor/banking relationships
* JV and alliance partners
* Sales, marketing, and branding strategies
* Customer relationship management systems
* Web 2.0 branding and overall networking good practices

Intellectual property

* Patents
* Copyrights
* Trademarks
* Trade secrets
* Trade dress
* Business processes (patentable)

Human assets

* Investment in the development, advancement, and interchangeability of workforce (career paths and satisfaction challenge)
* Skill and expertise of workforce (competence and experience)
* Special certifications, awards, industry recognition, security clearances
* Functionality and performance of teams
* Commitment, motivation, attitude, and loyalty to the institutional values
* Problem-solving skills
* Creativity and commitment to innovation
* Empowerment and access to resources

Practices and routines assets

* Know-how and show-how (codified in manuals and informal procedures and tacit rules on work plans)
* Systems and processes
* Information transmission, flow, and management
* Knowledge, management capture, and communication of best practices
* Training systems
* Ability to adapt to changes in management or the marketplace
* Ability to adjust practices for global market presentation

2. **Current View.** IP assets should not be used merely for defensive purposes but should also be viewed as an important asset and profit center that is capable of being monetized and generating value through licensing fees and other channels and strategies, *provided* that time and resources are devoted to uncovering these opportunities—especially dormant IP assets that do not currently serve at the heart of the company's current core competencies or focus (*proactive/systemic approach*).

3. **Future View.** IP assets are *the* premiere drivers of business strategy within the company and encompass human capital, structural/organizational capital, and customer/relationship capital. IAM systems need to be built and continuously improved to ensure that IP assets are used to protect and defend the company's strategic position in domestic and global markets and to create new markets, distribution channels, and revenue streams in a capital-efficient manner to maximize shareholder value (*core focus/strategic approach*).

CEOs and business leaders of companies of all sizes are often guilty of committing a serious strategic sin: failure to properly protect, mine, and harvest the company's intellectual property. This is especially true at many technology-driven and consumer-driven companies. During the dot.com and Web 1.0 Internet boom from 1997 to 2001, billions of dollars went into the venture capital and private equity markets, and the primary use of these proceeds by entrepreneurs was the creation of intellectual property and other intangible assets. Ten years later, however, emerging growth and middle-market companies have failed in many cases to leverage this intellectual capital into new revenue streams, profit centers, and market opportunities because of a singular focus on the company's core business or a lack of the strategic vision or expertise needed to uncover or identify other applications or distribution channels.

Entrepreneurs and growing company leaders may also lack the proper tools to understand and analyze the value of the company's intellectual assets. As discussed in Chapter 1, Professor Baruch Lev has discovered that only 15 percent of the "true intrinsic value" of the S&P 500 was found to be captured in their financial statements. Given the resources of an S&P 500 company, it is likely that smaller companies have their intangible assets even more deeply embedded, and the number for privately held companies may be as low as 5 percent. Imagine the consequences and opportunity cost if you were to prepare to eventually sell your business (or even structure an investment with a venture capitalist or strategic investor) and 95 percent of your inherent value got left on the table! This gap in capturing and reflecting this hidden value points out the critical need for a legal and strategic analysis of an emerging company's intellectual property portfolio.

The inversion of the ratio of tangible to intangible assets as a percentage of total company value has been dramatic. In 1978, tangible assets (e.g., property, plant, equipment, inventory) made up approximately 80 percent of the value of a typical Standard & Poor's 500 stock index company. By 2002, this was reduced to 20 percent of the total value, and the numbers continue to drop, especially in a Web-centric, virtual world. Today, for small- to mid-size enterprises (SMEs), the ratio of intangible to tangible assets can be as high as 8 or 10 to 1.

The harvesting of intellectual capital is a *strategic process* that must begin with the taking of an inventory by the company's management team and qualified outside advisers in order to get a comprehensive handle on the scope, breadth, and depth of the company's intangible assets. In these times of distrust and disappointment by shareholders in the management teams and boards of publicly held companies, corporate leaders have an obligation toward these shareholders to uncover hidden value and make the most of the assets that have been developed with corporate resources. The leadership of the company will never know whether it has a "Picasso in the basement" unless it both takes the time to inventory what's hiding in the basement and has a qualified intellectual capital inventory team capable of distinguishing between a Picasso and your children's art project. Once these assets are properly identified, an intellectual asset management system should be developed to ensure open communication and strategic management of these assets. At that point, the company is ready to engage in the strategic planning process to determine how to convert these assets into profitable revenue streams and new opportunities that will enhance and protect shareholder value. *IAM helps growing companies ensure that strategic growth opportunities are recognized, captured, and harvested into new revenue streams and markets.*

Dow Chemical is one company that has purposefully focused on intellectual capital to create a more efficient and profitable business. The company spends more than $1 billion a year in R&D and has more than 4,000 R&D staff. It owns 25,000 patents, which cost $30 million a year to maintain and support. By creating and using an IAM system, Dow was able to integrate its intellectual assets into its business strategy. Its first step was to survey its current processes to understand what was in place and what deficiencies existed. Next, it built a team of committed full-time management to develop and implement the business processes that could maximize its intellectual capital.

The process consisted of five stages: portfolio, classification, strategy, valuation and competitive assessment, and investment. Each patent's properties were identified, a cost center responsible for the upkeep of the active patents was assigned, a business group within Dow that benefited from the patent was identified, and each patent was classified as currently being used or likely to be used in the future. Dow's intellectual asset managers and IAM teams were thus able to identify gaps in the portfolio that allowed them to invest in new patents, eliminate cost by getting rid of unneeded patents, and gain revenues from licensing patents or gaining tax deductions by donating patents to charities. Dow's management of its intellectual assets, specifically patents, allowed it to reduce its maintenance costs by $40 million over the life of the patents and by $1 million in the first year alone. The company was able to increase its licensing from $25 million in 1994 to $125 million in 2004, and it was more than $150 million in 2009 on a total R&D investment that year of $1.6 billion.

Dow's IAM strategy, which is applicable to any product and/or service, is summarized in Figure 4-2.

We can also learn from Rank Xerox, the 80 percent–owned

Figure 4-2. The IAM strategic evaluation process.

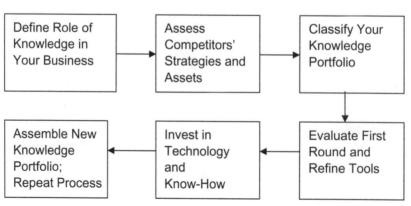

selling arm of Xerox, which undertook an internal "best practices" review of its sales staff. Team members gathered valuable global sales data and made country-by-country comparisons. After several weeks, Rank Xerox identified eight cases in which sales staff in individual countries dramatically outperformed their peers. Xerox studied these sales divisions (e.g., France and Switzerland) as best-practices candidates and made them an internal benchmark class. After site visits to the offices in the benchmarked countries to find out how the business was done, the team developed a book for each country's sales and service managers that showed what each benchmark was, how their territory compared with it, and how the top performer's system worked. After the implementation of the best-practice system, Rank Xerox sales exceeded budget by 5 percent.

Another company that reaped the rewards of implementing an IAM system that identifies, gathers, organizes, and shares employees' knowledge is Chevron. The company's former CEO, Kenneth T. Derr, focused his efforts on building a learning organization by sharing and managing knowledge throughout the company, which was one of the keys to reducing Chevron's operating costs by more than $2 billion per year. Similarly, British Telecom achieved success when the sales team used the briefings generated by a new knowledge management system to generate approximately $1.5 billion in new business.

The Strategic Benefits of Intellectual Asset Management

* **Employee reward, retention, and motivation.** People will be more loyal and more productive when working for an organization that empowers them, appreciates them, and rewards them for their innovative and creative contributions.

(continues)

* **Enhanced consumer loyalty.** The company's brand is strengthened when it is perceived as a thought leader that puts its brain power to work to create better products and services that enhance the lives of its consumers.

* **Better accountability for revenues.** IAM helps officers and directors meet their fiduciary duties to shareholders by creating accountability and internal controls over the allocation of R&D budgets and the tangible results that these initiatives may yield.

* **Strengthened risk management programs.** IAM helps reduce the risk of infringement actions, increases IP compliance in meeting filing deadlines to protect and preserve intangible corporate assets, and raises awareness (via training) of the proper internal handling and care of intangible assets.

* **Enhanced competitive advantage.** IAM raises the bar and barriers to entry by optimization of the roll-out of new products and services to keep the company a step ahead of its current and potential competitors.

* **More profitable financial performance.** IAM unlocks hidden or underperforming intangible assets and transforms them into profitable revenue streams and helps drive overall shareholder value.

* **Improved operational efficiency.** IAM helps leaders better manage and prioritize research and innovation initiatives and budgets, yielding better decision making, stronger channels, and more accurate internal and external financial reporting and operational controls.

Building an Effective IAM System

Over the past few years, a wide range of global solution providers have stepped to the plate in an attempt to automate the IAM process. These software tools facilitate knowledge management,

communication, collaboration, progress reports, resource allocation, management of outside advisers, infringement analysis, IP
department operations reports, budgeting, business planning,
benchmarking and metrics, reward and recognition programs,
research and analytics, training and educational tools, and a wide
range of related reports. In selecting a vendor, develop a Request
for Proposal (RFP) that is custom tailored to meet your company's needs and that complements other systems that you may
already have in place. Interview key stakeholders and future users
of these software and systems to determine their real day-to-day
needs and ensure that you are not paying for a lot of features
that are unnecessary and will be grossly underutilized.

Some vendors offer basic intellectual asset property management (IAPM) packages, which focus on docket management and
facilitate updates and communication between the company and
its outside counsel on the status of and deadlines for various
initial or renewal filings. As your portfolio of intellectual property
grows, you will want to have this type of system in place at a
bare minimum. But basic docket management software is the
minimum baseline that a growing or established company needs
to maintain and is limited to reports on the status of your intangible "inventory" at a given place or time. *Intellectual capital agrarians should put in place systems that are significantly more dynamic,
robust, and proactive to drive shareholder value and uncover new opportunities.* These systems are more likely to facilitate the kinds of
cross-functional brainstorming, budgeting, collaboration, project
awareness, resource allocations, monetization strategies, invention claim management and evaluation, competitive intelligence
tools, licensing transaction overpayment (inbound/outbound),
infringement analysis, and mapping that will not only ensure that

opportunities are maximized but also help you avoid wasteful duplication of effort or misallocation of resources and reduce the risks of costly litigation.

In selecting a vendor and an effective system for your company, conduct due diligence, talk to key contacts at other companies that already have systems in place (e.g., Ford, Microsoft, 3M, Honeywell, Cisco, IBM, P&G, GE), and read some of the reviews and white papers evaluating vendors and systems that are available on the websites of *IAM* magazine (www.iam-maga zine.com), IPMall (www.ipmall.info), and *CIO* magazine (www .cio.com).

The following vendors are active in these areas, and their websites offer insights about the features of their systems, as well as some of the criteria you should consider in making a selection:

* SAP (www.sap.com)
* Delphion (www.delphion.com)
* Lecorpio (www.lecorpio.com)
* MindMatters (www.us-mindmatters.com)
* Anaqua (www.anaqua.com)
* AIM-Harpoon (www.aim-harpoon.com)
* Artesia Technologies (www.artesia.com)

As with the acquisition of any critical software system, the variables and metrics you should evaluate in making a decision include costs, service and support, training, data migration, security and protection, ease of access and use, available mobile applications, alignment and compatibility with other systems, replacement costs, stability and credibility of vendor, custom applications, troubleshooting, reliability and system downtime, global use and language variations, IT staffing support requirements (in addition to those hosted at the cost of the vendor), data storage capabilities, project management capabilities, accessibility from a variety of Web browsers, timetable for installation and implementation, scalability, date architecture, hardware costs, searching and reporting capabilities, hosted (rather than on-premises) systems, and, of course, the "intangibles"—are your creative innovators "energized and content" with the selection you make?

For IAM systems analyses, and other related resources, you may want to visit the websites of these member-driven organizations:

* International Intellectual Property Institute (www.iipi.org)
* Intellectual Property Owners Association (www.ipo.org)
* American Intellectual Property Law Association (www.aipla .org)
* World Intellectual Property Organization (www.wipo.org)
* Licensing Executives Society (www.les.org)
* International Trademark Association (www.inta.org)
* National Collegiate Inventors and Innovators Alliance (NCIIA) (www.nciia.org)

Additional information regarding these organizations and other resources is included in the Resource Directory in the Appendix.

A strategic review of your current IAM practices should ask the following questions:

* What IAM systems, procedures, and teams are currently in place?
* How and when were these systems developed?
* Who is responsible or accountable for managing these systems within the company?

* To what degree are adequate systems for internal and external communication and collaboration now in place?

* What ideas/technology-harvesting filters and procedures for innovation decisional analysis (e.g., whether to move forward, budget allocation, timetable) are currently in place?

* Are the strategy and the process for harvesting and leveraging intellectual assets reactive or proactive?

* What are the real or perceived internal (politics, red tape, budgeting processes, organizational structure) and/or external (market conditions, rapid changes in the state of the art, competitor's strategies) hurdles that stand in the way of better IAM practices and procedures?

* What can be done to remove or reduce those barriers?

Conducting an IP Audit

The first step in developing an effective IAM system is to conduct an intellectual property (IP) audit to be led by outside legal and strategic advisers working in tandem with the internal R&D and innovation team. The IP audit is a multidisciplinary process that gathers data and takes inventory of all of the company's intellectual property assets so that they can then be managed and leveraged properly and profitably.

An IP audit can also include a competitive assessment of the strength and depth of the company's inventory of intellectual assets relative to those of the companies with which it competes, directly, indirectly, and perhaps down the road. This holistic competitive assessment may be especially critical if a future capital formation or merger/acquisition transaction is anticipated, during which these may become cultural issues in due diligence valuation.

In addition, the IP audit can be a useful tool to determine

where future research and development dollars or branding budgets should be allocated, especially if the company is losing competitive position to others or there are noticeable holes or dangerous weaknesses in its IP portfolio. As the intellectual capital agrarian matures, his or her inventory of intellectual assets should be getting stronger and deeper, not more shallow, in order to protect the company's market position and to enable it to continue to deliver and maintain its brand, reputation, trust, and value proposition in the management of its relationship with customers, suppliers, and channel partners.

The IP audit has seven primary phases, ranging from data gathering to the development of policies and procedures. There is a wide range of issues and action items that needs to be addressed during each phase, depending on the results of the audit and overall IP objectives. The seven phases are these:

1. **Inventory IP assets.** What categories of intangible assets does the company own?
2. **Organize IP assets.** Should the company build database/tracking and organizational core business models?
3. **Confirm/clarify IP ownership.** Does the company properly own/license all IP that is critical to its core business model?
4. **Verify IP legal protection and compliance.** Is the IP properly registered and protected under international, federal, and state laws?
5. **Evaluate IP policies and procedures.** Are internal and external stakeholder policies and procedures manuals and guidelines in place to ensure proper protection and usage of IP assets?
6. **Examine IP leveraging strategies.** What are the ways to leverage the company's IP assets into new opportunities and revenue streams?
7. **Assess IP enforcement strategies.** Is the company aware of any infringements of its IP, and what is its litigation strategy for moving forward?

A strategic planning process coupled with IAM systems in place will help you and your team uncover opportunities for growth. Key questions include:

* What patents, systems, and technologies have non-competing applications that could be licensed to third parties to create new revenue streams, joint ventures, or partnering opportunities, distribution channels, or profit centers?

* What brands lend themselves to extension licensing or co-branding opportunities?

* What distribution channels or partnering opportunities can be strengthened if the company has greater control or provided additional support and services to the channel?

* What types of different growth and expansion strategies are being used by the company's competitors? Why?

* Where are the strategic/operational gaps in the company's current licensing and alliance relationships?

As you can see from Figure 4-3, the strategic planning process helps identify the different *types* of protectable intellectual property and the ways in which it can be leveraged into new opportunities.

Measuring the Results of Innovation

Leaders of companies around the world who take their fiduciary responsibilities to shareholders seriously must be accountable for demonstrating results from the R&D dollars that are budgeted each year. Much has been written about how (and whether) innovation can be measured. Which components of innovation

Figure 4-3. Harvesting revenue streams and growth opportunities from your inventory of intellectual assets.

Protectable Types of Intellectual Property		Possible New Opportunities and Revenue Sources
• Patents • Trademarks (including brands and slogans) • Copyrights • Trade dress • Trade secrets • Distribution channels • Show-how and know-how • Website design and content/Web 2.0 strategies • Customer and strategic partner relationships • Proprietary processes and systems • Knowledge and technical workers	⇨	• New independent ventures • Joint ventures • Licensing • Outright sale • Co-branding • Franchising • New domestic markets • New ancillary products • Licenses • Strategic partnerships • Cooperatives, consortiums • Outsourcing • International expansion • Government contracts

can be quantitatively measured, and which are intangible? Which metrics are more relevant than others and in what context and for what situations?

Innovation metrics are difficult to define and to track with quantitative methods only. The most popular method for measuring innovation lately has been the return on investment (ROI), but the challenge is that it does not indicate whether this revenue is profitable or whether it will open up new avenues of innovation. In short, this method for measuring innovation does not tell how the product truly, directly or indirectly, affects the bottom line.

Another challenge is that almost all metrics are looking back in time after time and effort have already been exported. Intellectual capital agrarians need better tools, metrics, services, and filters that they can use effectively to predict results and avoid costly blunders. A wide variety of tools and metrics can be used to develop a shareholder value–driven internal methodology to ensure that innovation budgets are properly developed and assets efficiently harvested, as set forth in Figure 4-4.

Also, it is largely ineffective to measure innovation the same way you would ongoing product development. Companies have little experience in determining suitable metrics for innovation. Metrics can be one-sided, such as tracking patent submission while ignoring nonpatentable innovations. Some specific metrics can be misleading, such as the volume of ideas generated from an idea management initiative. Companies need to focus on the volume-quality balance, not on volume alone.

Key Quantitative Metrics in Measuring Innovation

There is also a wide range of strategic financial metrics that are commonly used as a basis for measuring the results of innovation (see Figure 4-5). These include:

* **Revenue growth from new products.** This is the most widely used metric by leading firms. It is based on strategic targets set by the business and an understanding of how the company can achieve its growth targets.

* **Patent submission.** An increasingly popular approach, this is widely abused by many companies outside the high-tech and pharmaceutical industries. Patents are only one form of pro-

Figure 4-4. Tools for measuring success and value enhancement.

Financial Tools	**IP Legal Tools**	**Customer Tools**
• Revenue Generation • Increments/Margin Improvement and Enhancement • Durability of Income Streams • PRPI (Profitable Revenue for Innovator) • Return on Intangible Assets	• # of new registered patents • # of new registered brands • # of new registered copyrights **R&D Tools** • # of successful discoveries (breakthrough vs. incremental) • ABC Rate (Alpha to Beta to Customer) • Effectiveness of R&D Alliances • Time to market analysis • Extended product life cycles	• # of new customers • Deepening and widening of existing customer relationship (and more dynamic intervention using customer user groups, advisory councils, etc.) • Increases in customer satisfaction and loyalty • Lead conversion rates • After-market support

Marketplace Tools	**Information Tools**	**HR Tools**
• Increases in market share • Increases in new barriers to entry • Improvement and enhancement of brand recognition/value • Strengthening in positioning as an innovative corporate citizen	• IAM Systems • Overall IT Efficiency and Knowledge Management/Best Practices • CRM System Improvement **Relationship Tools** • Strengthening of channel partner relationships • Strengthening of investing and lending relationships (capital market preceptors) • Supply chain efficiency	• Improvements in Employee Loyalty and Satisfaction (reduced turnover) • Enhancement of Employee Productivity and Motivation • Organizational Structural Streamlining and Accountability (Chief Innovation Office) • Technical and Scientific Advisory Boards (External/Internal)

tectable intellectual property, and many companies focus more on the legal aspects of protection than on the business upside.

   * **Idea submission and flow.** Ideas flowing through an idea management system provide a visible reference point to the volume and quality of submissions.

Figure 4-5. Top-rated 23 metrics to measure innovation.

Metric	Value
Customer satisfaction with products/service features	61.9%
R&D spending as a percentage of revenue	47.1%
% revenue/sales/gross margin from NP/services	44.4%
Time to market for new products/services	44.3%
Use of cross-functional teams	44.2%
Number of innovation initiatives funded	43.7%
Revenue growth (year to year)	42.4%
Order fulfillment cycle time	41.7%
Time to profitability for new products/services	40.9%
Avg time to act on identified business exposure/opp'ty	40.7%
On-time delivery	40.5%
Customer retention	40.2%
Growth rate in share of key customers' purchases	40.2%
Growth rate in number of customers	39.4%
Cost reduction	39.0%
Return on investment for new products/services	38.8%
Employee satisfaction	38.4%
Customer sat with order taking, scheduling, & delivery	37.8%
Profit growth (year to year)	36.5%
Employee productivity (revenue per FTE)	36.1%
% products/services making up 80% of sales volume	35.1%
% NP/services making up 80% of sales volume	34.0%
Number of patents	33.0%

✻ **Innovation capacity.** Companies measure innovation capacity using survey tools, such as the Innovation Climate Questionnaire or other qualitative tools, to determine whether the company has become more innovative.

At the end of the day, effective IAM systems and innovation metrics must drive and enhance shareholder value, typically in the following ways:

* **Creating high-margin income streams** (from licensing, franchising, and alliances)
* **Positioning the brand as an innovator to target markets**
* **Providing first/best/fastest to market/first mover advantage**
* **Setting up real, durable, and sustainable barriers to competition** (commitment to innovate better and smarter than the pack; government-granted contracts, patents, approvals [FDA])
* **Creating a more robust pipeline for new and innovative products and services** (momentum/magnetism for new markets)
* **Developing a loyal and productive workforce that views rewards as aligned with expectations and intrapreneurial career/ownership opportunities**
* **Earning the respect and admiration of industry peers, trade groups, and academics**
* **Establishing dynamic and deeper strategic relationships with customers, vendors, suppliers, channel partners (increasing in loyalty and reducing turnovers/drain rates)**
* **Increasing the ability to recruit and retain the most skilled and creative workforce**
* **Profiting from synergies and R&D efficiencies created by partnering, alliances, and acquisitions**
* **Establishing leadership teams and governance systems deducted to innovation, technological advancement, overall societal gain, and lifestyle enhancement** (GE's "Better Things for Life")
* **Aligning innovation results generated with overall organizational strategic goals and objectives** (R&D/innovation portfolio alignment)

CHAPTER 5

Building Fences to Protect Your Turf: Developing a Legal Strategy

Confiding a secret to an untrustworthy person is like carrying a bag of grain to the market with a hole in the bottom.
—African Proverb

Farmers and ranchers build fences around their property to delineate what property belongs to them, to prevent intruders from stealing their crops, and to prevent cattle from wandering off their property. Fences protect what is theirs and tell the outside world where the lines of trespass are. In the intangible asset-, knowledge-, and information-driven society, intellectual property laws can serve as virtual fences. We use these laws to declare to

93

the world which intangible properties belong to us and where the lines of infringement have been drawn. We choose, as a matter of strategy, policy, and ethics, where to build tall concrete walls rather than barbed-wire fences or wooden split-rail-style posts, which can be seen through and are relatively easy to penetrate. Our budget constraints, our attitudes toward intangibles, our degree of expertise and experience in harvesting intellectual assets, and the size and scope of our inventory of properties are all relevant variables in dictating which types of fences should be deployed for which of our properties.

The intellectual capital agrarian must make the same choices that his or her agricultural brothers made 200 years ago. Do I share my proprietary farming best practices, know-how, systems, protocols, tools, networks, relationships, methodologies, channels, and strategies with my fellow farmers, or do I keep these assets hidden and protected behind guarded walls? If I do share them with others, then at what price and pursuant to which business model do I do so? As a consultant? As a trainer? As a vendor? As a licensor? As a franchisor? As a joint venture or alliance partner? As an acquirer? To what extent does this knowledge truly provide a competitive advantage over other farmers? If it does in fact do so, does it apply to all types of farmers? Or only to my direct competitors? To what extent could this knowledge or these best practices be useful to nonfarmers in other businesses? Can I build business models to sell or license this knowledge outside the agricultural community? In other domestic markets? Abroad?

The key questions have never changed, but the crops have evolved over time. Decisions regarding potatoes and tomatoes still exist, but the commodity under the biggest global strategic microscope today is the crop of knowledge, which can manifest itself in many different ways. Companies of all sizes and in all industries, from early-stage entrepreneurs to midmarket gazelles to established global conglomerates, are *all* challenged with the exact same question: *How can we be effective and efficient farmers as we plant and harvest our intellectual capital, and which are the best fences to protect our turf?*

So what's really at stake? Why should you care about the legal trends and strategies affecting the protection of your intellectual assets? Consider the following data (no matter which side of the fence you are on):

* About 3,000 new patent infringement cases are filed in the United States each year, more than double the average number of cases 15 years ago.

* The average cost of patent litigation in the United States (per case, per party) is $3 million to $10 million, and each case takes up to five years to come to fruition, longer if there is an appeal, according to 2010 reports of the American Intellectual Property Law Association (AIPLA). Trademark litigation and other types of IP-related disputes run between $1 million and $2 million, depending on the costs of expert witnesses, market research, and other evidentiary tools needed to prove dilution, confusion, and damages.

* Today, counterfeiting is a global enterprise—a rapidly growing problem in numerous industries around the world. Revenues from sales of counterfeit goods are estimated to have grown by more than 400 percent since the early 1990s, while sales of legitimate goods grew by just 50 percent. According to a 2009 report from the FBI, counterfeiting now costs U.S. companies some $200 to $250 billion annually. With counterfeit goods

accounting for approximately 5 to 7 percent of world trade, it is hardly hyperbole when the FBI tags counterfeiting "the crime of the twenty-first century."

* In 2002 (the most recent year for which data are available), the U.S. Department of Justice reported 8,254 civil cases related to the theft of intellectual property. This figure does not include the tens of thousands of cases filed at the state level for misappropriation and breaches of confidentiality agreements or covenants not to compete. In competitive and recessionary times, corporate espionage and theft are likely to have risen significantly, and the steps you take to protect your intellectual assets and the decisions you make as to the porousness of your fence posts have significant legal, strategic, and financial implications on the future growth and direction of your company.

* In 2009, there were more than 5,000 companies in the United States that spent between $50,000 and $100,000 per month on intellectual property litigation costs, according to a study by Litigation Risk Management, Inc. Some of these costs are reimbursed by intellectual capital infringement insurance policies (if you can get them), and many costs are simply direct hits to the company's bottom line.

There are various types of fences available to your company, each with strategic advantages and disadvantages. Understand that there is no one best or right choice. Each company must decide for itself which types of fences it wants to build and which will best serve its stakeholders, from the open architecture platform of Linux to the closely guarded code at Microsoft, from the high concrete walls around the trade-secreted formula for Coca-Cola to the community-driven and transparent Wikipedia. It is up to the leaders of the company to draw the lines in the sand and to work with in-house lawyers and external law firms to choose the legal strategies that will drive shareholder value and help ensure future harvests that are timely and bountiful. The level of proprietary intellectual property protection for which you are eligible (and that you choose to enforce) will have a direct effect on your business models, your pricing strategies, your channel loyalty, and your ability to license the technology on brands and on profit margins. And your IP protection and harvesting strategies may evolve over time as market conditions and technology evolve. See the accompanying feature on Kodak for an excellent case study that supports this reality.

Eastman Kodak: A Tale of Many Fences

It would be hard to imagine a company that has had to change its fences as many times as Eastman Kodak over the past 20 years. The 130-year-old company enjoyed an incredible history as the dominant player in the film industry for more than 100 years, and its worldwide recognized brands and technology served as a fence driving 85 percent of its revenues and 100 percent of its very high margin profits. But in a world that seemed to shift to digital almost overnight and with most citizens armed with multiple digital cameras in their pockets at any given moment, the company quickly achieved dinosaur status by the early 2000s.

Kodak began to search for new product lines—some say way too late in the game—and has focused on the consumer and home printing industry since 2006, but that niche is highly competitive and may not be profitable for Kodak until 2012 or 2013. So, with its main crops dying on the vine (camera film) and it new crops facing margin wars, the leadership of the company turned to its most valuable assets, which had been sitting under the cushion the

(continues)

entire time—its digital media patents—as a source of revenues and profits. These early-rediscovered fences could be used as swords, not just shields to generate revenues and drive shareholder value. And, in fact, Kodak settled lawsuits in 2009 against Samsung and LG for $550 million and $400 million, respectively—a bigger crop, indeed!

In June 2010, Kodak announced that it would focus on building a different type of fence. It had grown tired of the massive legal fees and of the potentially negative publicity about its being a patent "lion," and it now wants to be a patent-milking cow as a licensor. CEO Antonio Perez has shifted his focus to intellectual property licensing as a key source of revenue and profits, mainly focusing on Kodak's significant inventory of digital media patents, while still trying to gain market share in the competitive field of consumer home printers and through Prosper Press, a new initiative aimed at publishers and catalog makers that sells high-end printers at $1.5 million to $4 million per unit—a pricier and high-end crop aimed at a narrow and shrinking market. Only the future will tell us whether the transformed business model and retooled strategic focus will be effective, but clearly this company has been an intellectual capital agrarian for nearly 14 decades and isn't going down without a fight.

Legal Management of Intellectual Property

The legal and strategic management of the company's intellectual property typically falls into the following key categories:

* **Ideation and Development:** Steps taken at the early stages of a project to ensure that proper protection is in place at both the enterprise and the employee (or outside contractor/adviser) levels.

* **Prosecution and Registration:** Steps taken to file for the ownership of the intellectual properties with government agencies at the domestic and global levels.

* **Patent Mapping and Competitive Intelligence:** Steps taken to both avoid claims of infringement by third parties and to define the scope of exclusivity and competitive advantage that a company can enjoy from its intangible assets.

* **Maintenance and Enforcement:** Steps taken and systems put in place to ensure that intellectual property assets are properly maintained, registrations kept current, and proactive steps taken to pursue infringers. It is critical to be proactive in the enforcement of your company's rights or they could be lost or weakened due to inaction or complacency. As coach Vince Lombardi was famous for saying, "The best defense is a good offense."

* **Transactional and Revenue Generation:** Steps taken by the legal department and/or outside counsel that serve as a strategic liaison to the business teams responsible for intellectual property–driven transactions and revenue-generating activities, such as those discussed in Chapter 8.

The Allocation of Legal Budgets

Intellectual capital agrarians must make critical strategic decisions about how and where legal and IAM system budgets will be allocated. Some focus on protecting the core and others on facilitating new ideas and innovation pipelines. It is critical to monitor how legal fees are broken down between new IP filings and global prosecution costs, IP infringement management costs (as either plaintiff or defendant), and IP transactional costs relating to intellectual capital harvesting and monetization strategies. The pie charts in Figure 5-1 demonstrate the differences in budget and strategic approaches.

Figure 5-1. The different approaches to IP protection legal budgeting.

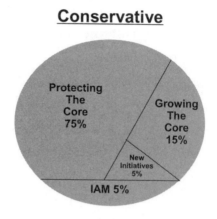

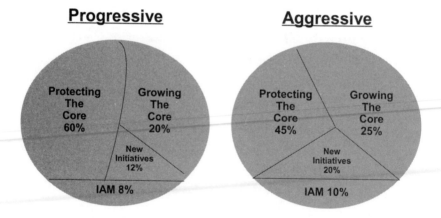

Understanding Intellectual Property Laws

Our intellectual property laws are deeply rooted in our nation's legal system. Patents and copyrights are addressed in Article I, Section 8, of the U.S. Constitution. Our founding fathers clearly felt that rights in property could be both tangible and intangible and deserved to be protected. We are one of the few nations on the planet to address intellectual property laws in a founding charter. Were our founding fathers so visionary that they knew that these assets would be key strategic drivers of our economy more than 200 years later? Or were they primarily farmers, inventors, and entrepreneurs who simply understood the timeless premise of protecting and harvesting one's crops, in whatever form they may take?

In Figure 5-2, the branches of intellectual property law in the United States (and many other countries) are depicted. The sections that follow offer a brief overview of aspects of U.S. intellectual property laws. (For a more detailed discussion of the specifics of intellectual property law, see Chapter 8 of my book *Franchising and Licensing: Two Powerful Ways to Grow Your Business in Any Economy*, 4th edition [AMACOM, 2011].)

Figure 5-2. Branches of intellectual property.

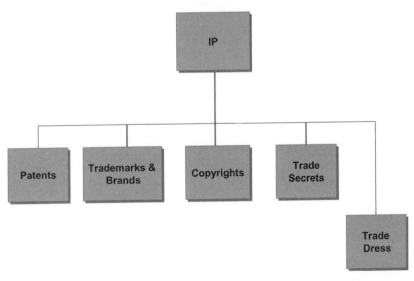

Patents

A patent grants an inventor the right to exclude others from making, using, selling, or offering to sell his invention throughout the United States or from importing the invention into the United States for a limited period of time. To obtain a patent, an application must be submitted with the U.S. Patent and Trademark Office (known as the "USPTO"). As an intellectual capital agrarian, you can use patents both offensively and defensively—either as a fence to defend your turf and market share or as a weapon to attack others who may be trespassing on your proprietary farm. Patents can also be used as a strategic tool to generate new revenue streams from licensing and to obtain access to other technologies via cross-licensing or patent pooling. A patent for an invention will not be granted if the subject matter of the claimed invention was publicly used or on sale in the United States by anyone, including the inventor, more than one year before the effective filing date of the application or if the subject matter of the claimed invention was patented by anyone, anywhere in the world, more than one year before the effective filing date of the U.S. application.

Four categories of patents are available:

1. **Utility Patents.** This is the most common of the four categories. Utility patents protect a new and useful process, machine, manufacture, or composition of matter, or any new and useful improvement thereto, for a period of 20 years from the filing date of the application.

2. **Design Patents.** These patents protect the visual ornamental characteristics embodied in or applied to an article of

manufacture, not its utilitarian features, for a period of 14 years from the date the patent is granted.

3. **Plant Patents.** The least used of the four categories, these patents are issued to protect certain new varieties of plants that have been asexually reproduced for a term of 20 years from the filing date of the application.

4. **Business Method Patents.** This category of patents discloses and claims new methods of doing business. A business method may be defined as a method of operating any aspect of an economic enterprise. The appropriateness of patenting business methods has been the subject of numerous court actions over the years. For many years, the USPTO took the position that "methods of doing business" were not patentable. But, with the increased popularity of the Internet, many ways of doing business in cyberspace began to be viewed as novel and patentable, and it was no longer practical to determine whether a particular computer-implemented invention was a technological invention or a business invention. Novel methods of business were deemed patentable in the late 1990s by the U.S. Circuit Court for the Ninth Circuit in the landmark case *State Street Bank v. Signature Financial Group, Inc.*, wherein the court found that Signature's patent for its "hub and spoke" mutual fund management process was valid.

In general, the patent application and registration process can last from two to five years and can be very costly. Therefore, before attempting to obtain a patent, an intellectual capital agrarian should conduct a strategic cost-benefit analysis to determine whether the benefits of being able to exclude others from making, using, or selling the invention outweigh the significant costs of prosecuting, maintaining, and protecting the patent. As part of this analysis, you should consider:

* Key trends in the marketplace

* Key trends in the capital markets

* The projected commercial value of the invention

* Out-of-pocket expenses to obtain the patent, including legal fees, advertising, marketing, and retooling costs

* The invention's proximity to existing patented and nonpatented technology (from an infringement and a commercial development perspective) owned by both competitors and strategic-alliance partners

* The ability to fully exploit the invention during the timeframe of exclusivity granted by a patent

* The market value and commercial usefulness of the invention two to five years down the road, after completion of the patent application process

* The availability of adequate strategic pathways for protecting the invention, such as trade secret law

Trademarks and Service Marks

Trademarks and service marks are words, names, symbols, or devices used to identify and distinguish the products or services of one company from those of another and to indicate the source of the products or services. A *trademark* identifies a product and is typically applied physically to the product or displayed on containers or labels for the product or on displays associated with the product. A *service mark* is used in the sale and advertising of various types of services and generally appears in advertising campaigns and in promotional materials.

Conventional wisdom suggests that trademark deployment

should be clear and consistent and reflect core values, with campaigns, slogans, and messaging being updated from time to time. Messaging for Intel has for more than 20 years focused on one thing—the speed of computing offered by its computer chips—while companies such as GEICO have over the years deployed multiple branding strategies. In early 2011, GEICO had four different branding campaigns running simultaneously (the gecko, the caveman, the money pole with bulging eyes, and the Rod Serling lookalike), which can be both entertaining and potentially confusing to the company's target audience(s). Logos can be trademarked (e.g., the seashell for Shell or the golden arches for McDonald's), as can the design aspects of a product, its configuration, its packaging, its color, its scents, its sounds, or its shipping containers. Advertising campaign taglines like "Where's the beef?" (Wendy's) or "Don't leave home without it" (American Express) have become so popular that they qualify as slogans for trademark protection.

Types of Marks

Not all words or phrases are entitled to trademark or service mark protection. The mark must, as a preliminary matter, identify the products or services as coming from a particular source. Marks that are generally protectable are those that are coined, fanciful, arbitrary, or suggestive. Generic marks are not protectable, and marks that are merely descriptive of the products or services they identify may not be protected without a showing of acquired distinctiveness or "secondary meaning."

Coined, fanciful, or arbitrary. This is the strongest category of mark that can be protected. The mark is either a coined word, such as Exxon, or a word in common usage that has no meaning when applied to the goods and services in question, such as Dove for dish detergent or body soap or Apple for computers. These marks are inherently distinctive and readily distinguish the products or services of one company from those of its competitors.

Suggestive. A suggestive mark requires the consumer to use some degree of imagination in determining what product or service is represented and, as such, is the next strongest category of mark that may be protected. Owners of suggestive marks are not required to establish secondary meaning. Examples of suggestive marks include Coppertone for suntan oil, Whirlpool for appliances, and Chicken of the Sea for tuna fish.

Descriptive. Marks that are descriptive of the goods or services they identify cannot be protected unless the manufacturer can establish that its mark has acquired distinctiveness. This requires demonstration that the public associates the particular mark with the goods or services of the specific producer (known as "secondary meaning"). This category includes marks (e.g., Holiday Inn for motels, Weight Watchers for weight loss centers, or Soft Soap for hand cleaner) that are descriptive but that are nevertheless registered because they have acquired distinctiveness.

Copyrights

The legal basis for copyright protection is found in the U.S. Constitution, which empowers Congress to enact legislation to promote the progress of science and the useful arts by securing for a limited period of time to authors the exclusive right to their respective creations. Copyright law has always been the legal "workhorse" that has struggled to keep pace with the speed of technological innovation to protect the rights of authors, artists, musicians, filmmakers, and others who rely on the sale of originally created works or data as their primary source of income.

Congress, pursuant to the power granted by the Constitution, enacted the Copyright Act, which provides protection to all "original works of authorship fixed in any tangible medium of expression." This definition includes not only literary materials but also pictorial, graphic, and sculptural works.

Protections Afforded to the Owner of Copyright

The Act provides that the owner of a copyright has the exclusive right to:

* Reproduce the work
* Prepare derivative works
* Distribute copies of the work
* Perform the work publicly
* Display the work publicly

The owner's copyright is infringed if any of these exclusive rights is violated.

A copyright protects only the expression of an idea, not the idea itself. That is, a copyright protects only the original labor of the author that gave substance to the idea, not the underlying abstract idea or concept of the author. Once the copyrightable work is created in a tangible form, it automatically enjoys federal copyright protection and may be transferred or licensed to others.

Work Made for Hire

Typically the author of the work is the owner of the copyright. Works developed by someone on behalf of another, however, may be considered "works made for hire." The Act defines a "work made for hire" as:

* A work prepared by an employee within the scope of his or her employment

* A work specially ordered or commissioned for use as a contribution to a collective work, as a part of a motion picture or other audiovisual work, as a translation, as a supplementary work, as a compilation, as an instructional text, as a test, as answer material for a test, "if the parties expressly agree in a written instrument signed by them that the work shall be considered a work made for hire."

A "work made for hire," therefore, must either be prepared by an "employee" or fit within one of the narrow categories listed here. With respect to agreements with independent contributors, if the work to be commissioned falls within one of the narrow enumerated categories, the agreement must clearly set forth that the work is intended by both parties to be a "work made for hire" under the Act and owned by the commissioning party. Absent such express written agreement, the work would be presumed to be owned by its creator, not the person who paid for its creation.

Compilation Copyrights

Intellectual capital agrarians can also claim certain rights for their efforts in assembling a series of works even if those works were authored by others under the concept known as the "compilation copyright." To register a copyright for a compilation, the new agrarian must ensure that (1) it has permission to utilize and create derivative works of all materials developed by parties other than itself, including those materials developed by others and adapted by the company, and (2) the original content developed by the intellectual capital agrarian represents a sufficient addition of original authorship to qualify for copyright protection in the compilation.

Copyright protection for a compilation extends only to incremental original expression (i.e., "nontrivial distinguishable variation" created by a sufficient "sweat of the brow" test) made by the author and not to the preexisting, underlying copyrighted material. Generally, the creation of original content or the exercise of editorial discretion in selecting certain articles, materials, or other copyrighted works over others for inclusion in a compilation and deciding in what order to present the selected works within the compilation (e.g., creating a "best of" or "most important" collection of articles) is sufficient to constitute "original authorship" necessary for registration of the compilation. To be copyrightable, a compilation work must be noninfringing, meaning that permission is required for use of the underlying or "compiled" works.

Trade Secrets

An intellectual capital agrarian's advantage over its competitors is gained and maintained in large part through its trade secrets and proprietary information. A company's trade secrets typically consist of its confidential formula, recipes, business format and plan, prospect lists, pricing methods, marketing and distribution techniques, key employee data, systems, processes, training manuals, pipeline reprints, partner demographics, and customer information.

Not all ideas and concepts are considered trade secrets.

Courts have generally set forth three requirements for information to qualify for trade secret protection:

* The information must have some commercial value.

* The information must not be generally known or readily ascertainable by others.

* The owner of the information must take all reasonable steps to maintain its secrecy. In order to preserve legal protections for its trade secrets, the company must follow a reasonable and consistent program for ensuring that the secrecy of the information is maintained.

There are many factors, however, in addition to these three, that courts have considered in deciding the extent to which protection should be afforded for trade secrets. Among those factors most often cited are:

* The extent to which the information is known by others outside the company

* The measures employed within the company to protect its secrets

* The value of the information to its owner, including the resources expended to develop the information

* The amount of effort that would be required by others to duplicate the effort or "reverse engineer" the technology

* The nature of the relationship between the alleged infringer/misappropriator and the owner of the trade secret

Trade secrets are typically protected either by duty or by contract—hence the need for confidentiality or nondisclosure agreements when proprietary information is shared with a third party that does not owe you any type of fiduciary obligation. Trade secret protection in the United States is governed primarily by state law, and court rulings vary from state to state. However, almost every state has some version of a law that makes the theft or unauthorized dissemination of a trade secret an unlawful act. At the federal level, theft of trade secrets can also result in criminal penalties under the Economic Espionage Act. High-profile cases typically arise when an executive of one company leaves for one of its competitors, as when Mark Hurd left Hewlett-Packard to join Oracle in 2010, and it is often alleged or presumed that certain proprietary information is leaving with him or her.

Trade Dress

Trade dress generally refers to characteristics of the overall visual and design appearance of a product, its packaging, or the interior decor of a restaurant or retail store or even the navigational features and design of a website. Trade dress may include external building features, interior designs, signage, uniforms, product packaging, and similar features designed to build brand awareness and to distinguish one company's products or services from those of another. Trade dress may be subject to protection if the combination of features used in the presentation, packaging, or "dress" of the goods and services is both nonfunctional and distinctive. Rights in trade dress are developed through actual and consistent use and through the consumer's recognition of their distinction. There are no registration processes at the state or federal level.

For example, in the 1992 case of *Taco Cabana International, Inc. v. Two Pesos, Inc.,* which was affirmed by the Supreme Court, a jury found the following combination of restaurant decor features to be protectable trade dress:

* Interior and patio dining areas decorated with artifacts, bright colors, paintings, and murals

* Overhead garage doors sealing off the interior from the patio areas

* Festive exterior paintings having a color scheme using top border paint and neon stripes:

* Bright-colored awnings and umbrellas

* A food-ordering counter set at an oblique angle to the exterior wall that communicates electronically with the food preparation and pickup areas

* An exposed food preparation area accented by cooking and preparation equipment visible to the consumer

* A condiment stand in the interior dining area proximate to the food pickup stand

This case, and others like it, suggests the increased availability of protection for nonfunctional components of systems, design processes, protocols, and operating strategies within the business.

Can This Business Model Be Sustained?

Kudos to those companies around the globe that aggressively enforce their intellectual capital rights and do not allow illegal trespass on their property. But can this strategy go too far? Will high fences and concrete walls be helpful in the short term in their effectiveness and yet do long-term harm in driving shareholder value? Texas Instruments in recent years has devoted significant resources to patent litigation and patent licensing, and the results have been impressive, netting the company more than $1 billion a year from litigation settlements and patent licenses as a result of vigilant enforcement policies. *In some years, revenues from these sources have exceeded net income from product sales.* Impressive, but dangerous. When revenues from litigation exceed revenues from innovation, this can be the beginning of the end of the future of the company. Yes, we must be diligent in building fences, but walls cannot be a strategic substitute for the output of the new products and services that are intended to come from within the company.

CHAPTER 6

Separating the Wheat from the Chaff: Readying Crops for the Market

A new idea is delicate. It can be killed by a sneer or a yawn; it can be stabbed to death by a joke or worried to death by a frown on the key person's face.

—CHARLES BROWDER

In the global field of intellectual capital agrarianism, why are there so many ineffective farmers and so few good ones? Why can't companies, governments, universities, nongovernmental organizations (NGOs), and trade associations do a better job harvesting their intellectual assets before they go stale or to waste? Why do so many crops rot and fail to drive shareholder value and why are so few brought to the marketplace? Why is so much of our global intellectual capital still sitting in someone's file cabinet or desk drawer, on someone's hard drive, or between someone's ears, with no hope of being released, embraced, exploited, or enjoyed? It's too easy to blame red tape, politics, turf wars, shifting strategic priorities, lack of vision, shrinking budgets, or cultural ignorance and make them the excuses for our global underleveraging of intellectual capital, though that may be the reason in many cases for the road block or speed bump in innovation and ideation. But surely it must be something deeper—a corporate mental block, a blind spot, an institutional complacency, an organizational inability to recognize or understand the assets it owns and that it has a fiduciary responsibility to its shareholders to properly harvest.

If we know *who* the better intellectual capital farmers are around the globe (DuPont, Google, Dow Chemical, IBM, 3M, Apple), then why can't the rest of us learn from their best practices, strategies, culture, customs, habits, and channels? Why are so few companies able to routinely convert the ideas of their employees, partners, and customers into durable and sustainable revenue streams, new markets, and profit centers? What processes, disciplines, and strategic screens and filters are the successful farmers using to gain competitive advantages over the inept farmers? What systems are used for resource allocation, budgeting, and funding R&D? What idea screens and selection processes have empowered these farmers to be significantly more successful than their competitors? How can your company adopt the use of similar tools, seed, irrigation, fertilizer, and pesticide to yield a more productive and profitable harvest? If cash is fertilizer, how and where should it be spread in the R&D and innovation budgeting and resource allocation process?

Some Best Practices and Common Mistakes

Why are a few companies successful at extracting shareholder value from their intellectual capital assets, while most are not? How can companies of all sizes and in all instances better optimize their innovation portfolios and achieve better returns on their innovation investments? Here are a few best practices and common mistakes to consider:

1. **Intellectual asset harvesting must be proactive not reactive, strategic not tacit, and rewarded not discouraged.** Google has perfected a culture of innovation where employees are rewarded and can even be penalized for falling asleep at the innovation wheel. At Google, leaders and managers foster innovation, but placing human skills as a priority over technical skills and accessibility is more important than authority. Leaders serve as mentors and coaches and are discouraged from being dictators and micromanagers. At Starbucks, Howard Schultz has retooled a more proactive strategy in an attempt to recapture the chain's heyday by redefining brands, business models, and customer value propositions. He recognizes that just because something worked in the past does not mean it will work in the future. Stagnation and complacency are the enemies of innovation and growth.

2. **Intellectual asset harvesting must be long term in its thinking, strategy, and approach.** At the peak of the recession in 2009, the leadership of the world's largest companies was changing every 18 months, causing an inability to set an innovation agenda or clear strategic direction about priorities and resource allocation. Innovation is a marathon, not a sprint, and companies and their governors and leaders must be patient yet

persistent in adopting a long-term view. Very few things of value can be built overnight.

3. **Companies must invest in the gathering, documentation, and codification of their intellectual assets.** For many companies, the know-how, show-how, processes, systems, and technical knowledge that drives their success often is undocumented and poorly managed. Internal best practices are shared over a water cooler and not captured and codified in an operations manual or training program. There also seems to be greater "institutional memory" over worst practices and failures than our best practices and successes. Knowledge leaves the premises every night as workers exit the building and some of it never returns.

Faced with this problem, Northrop Grumman's Air Combat Systems (ASC) decided to create a knowledge management procedure that will capture the tacit knowledge or know-how and experience locked in its employee' heads.[1] As its B-2 bomber program was winding down due to market demand shifts and because of anticipated downsizing, the Northrop Grumman ASC unit faced the potential of losing the precious knowledge and expertise needed to support and maintain its complex aircrafts that will be flying and carrying lives and cargos for years to come. Thus, ASC implemented procedures that will identify subject matter experts and capture their knowledge.

It conducted an audit that revealed that 75 percent of employees believe that knowledge in the discovery, development, and marketing of products they worked on was either very

---

1. Knowledge Management at Northrop Grumman by Megan Santosus, September 1, 2001, available at http://www.cio.com/article/30481/Knowledge_Management_at_Northrop_Grumman.

important or somewhat important. More importantly, 51 percent said the brains of ASC employees were the primary source for best practices and lessons learned, while 16 percent said electronic documents, 13 percent said e-mail, another 13 percent said electronic knowledge bases, and only 7 percent said paper documents.[2]

With almost half of the employees spending at least eight hours each week looking for information they needed to do their jobs, ineffective knowledge management was costing ACS an estimated $150 million annually. With these findings in mind, ACS devised a three-pronged strategy focusing on people, processes, and technology that included Web-based info-gathering sites and databases searchable by experts' names, field of expertise, or products. After employment levels settled, rather than using the system as a mode of retaining knowledge, Northrop Grumman began using it as a way to increase innovation and speed customer responsiveness.

4. **The selection of projects that move forward for implementation must be free from nepotism and favoritism.** As Oliver Schlake, a professor of innovation and entrepreneurship at the Smith School of Business at the University of Maryland, has said, "Pet Projects are resource draining cats with nine lives—they are virtually impossible to shut down and keep re-appearing at the doorstep." The process must be objective and aligned with overall business strategy (not personal agendas) in order to fully optimize the innovation portfolio. Intellectual capital agrarians should put processes in place to create impartial judges and juries who apply objective and well-published criteria, screens, and filters to determine which projects go to the next

---

2. Ibid.

level, which are put on the back burner, which will be developed externally and which should be discarded.

5. **The new product or service line must be properly plotted in the risk/reward matrix.** Intellectual capital agrarians need to build an accurate matrix of customer/market/product influencers, which may range from low risk/easy to adopt on the one extreme to high risk/difficult to understand on the other extreme. The plotting on the matrix will help dictate decisions regarding marketing campaigns, timetables, resources, and distribution channels. If a product is difficult to demonstrate and is perceived as radically new and high risk, it will have a low initial trialability rate. An example is the long adoption window that the Segway personal movers experienced in the 1990s, though they are now a widely accepted tool in mall and airport security and city tours. In contrast, products or services that are low risk or only incrementally new (e.g., Amazon's decision to start selling toys and music or Visa's introduction of branded affinity cards) are easy to test, easy to understand, and easy for consumers to adopt.

A Reality Test for Effective Agrarianism

Each year, approximately $1 trillion is spent in R&D around the globe by public and private companies, governments, universities, trade associations, foundations, individual inventors, research laboratories, and professional societies. But what revenues, profits, and innovation can be shown from all of that spending? How do we close the gap between dollars spent and dollars earned? And if we don't close the gap soon, will those dollars be allocated indefinitely? The United States fell from first to fifth in

R&D spending in 2009 and is likely to fall further if research cannot be harvested into revenue to drive stakeholder value or donor satisfaction. The U.S. Patent and Trademark Office estimates that the intellectual property in this country is worth well north of $5 trillion, but we fall short of harvesting those assets via commercialization and monetization to drive shareholder and social value.

So what variables contribute to a company's or organization's success or failure at intellectual capital training and harvesting? Let's look at questions that constitute a "reality test" for whether one is capable of being an effective agrarian:

* What is the role and importance of intellectual capital creation and monetization within the company? Where do they sit in the food chain of top board and CEO priorities and burning agendas? Are they truly a top priority, or do they live in a few windowless offices staffed by resource-starved scientists who will never have the proper tools and support to fertilize a strategic innovation field?

* From an internal reality perspective, what is the company or organization's *actual* capability to innovate? Has it placed a priority on recruiting and rewarding teams that are capable of breakthrough or incremental innovation? Do workers truly feel that innovating (rather than merely maintaining the status quo) is a critical component of their job description?

* From an external reality perspective, what competitive advantage can truly be gained via innovation? Are the company's industry and target market dominated by "me-toos," "copy-cats," "wanna-bes," "infringers," and "do-nothings," making it easier to join the pack train than to break out of it? Have consumers

demanded innovation as a condition of consuming, or are they just as complacent as their suppliers? What are the risks of complacency to both producer and consumer?

* What are the resource realities? Is there access to the resources required to plant and harvest a field of innovative crops? If yes, how should projects be screened and resources be allocated to drive and maximize shareholder value? If no, where can they be found? What capital markets, strategic partners, or governmental or foundational sources of capital or noncapital resources exist that may be available as strategic options?

* How do the stages of growth of the company, economic trends, product and service life cycles, fads, consumer loyalty, and channel strength all fit into the company's overall intellectual asset agrarian strategy? If it is committed to innovate, will a customer or a market still be open when it is ready to harvest? Or will they have passed the company by, given the time to market or product life-cycle challenges? Will the consumers' appetite be satiated by the time the company's fruits and vegetables are ready to make it to the dinner table? How relevant are the metrics of time and speed to market in the particular industry?

* Has the company built a culture that properly motivates people at all levels to be innovative and creative and work in cross-functional teams without politics or red tape?

* Has the company developed an internal system, such as the one depicted in Figure 6-1, that is customized to it and its industry to enable it to bring new products, services, and ideas to fruition? The process from ideation to product launch to profitability is long and tedious, with many steps along the way. Each step both represents an opportunity for driving shareholder value and offers the potential for project derailment.

Figure 6-1. The new product development cycle.

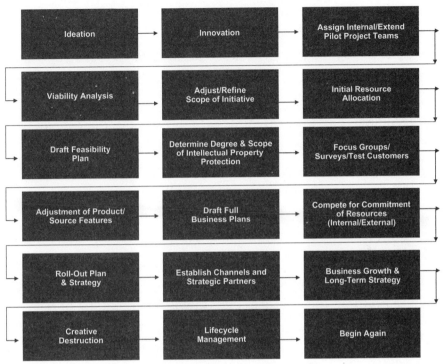

Inventor's Syndrome

Another key variable influencing how and why some companies are better than most others in harvesting intellectual capital is what I like to call the "inventor's syndrome." Being an intellectual capital agrarian is *not* about building a better mousetrap if nobody wants to pay for one and the ones available now work just fine. Thomas Edison, the most pragmatic inventor of modern times, was perpetually focused on inventing around consumer needs and an actual product, *not* for the sake of mere invention. The "oohs" and "aahs" of your scientific and academic peers may fuel your ego, but they will do little for your pocketbook.

123

More than a century ago, Edison said, "There is always a way to do things better. Find it." He lived by this principle. Most of Edison's inventions were improvements of existing technologies. Although he is known as the inventor of the light bulb, he did not actually invent the first one. Rather, he invented the first commercially practical incandescent light. Edison built on the contributions of other inventors over the previous three-quarters of a century and, together with his team, set out to create longer-lasting bulbs as a dedicated intellectual capital agrarian.

Another lesson to be learned from Edison's beliefs and actions is that the right mix of talent, ideas, and environment will birth inventions on a regular basis. In Edison's time, the general belief was that one could not simply plan to invent something; the act of invention is just the product of isolated genius. Edison proved them wrong. He demonstrated that, by bringing together people with a wide variety of skills to work in an open and collaborative environment with the purpose of building valuable marketable products, he was able to produce world-changing inventions. In fact, at his Invention Factory at Menlo Park, New Jersey, Edison and his staff of 200 set a goal to produce a minor invention every 10 days and a major one every six months. To turn research and development into real innovation and to brainstorm innovation into harvestable products, services, new markets, and profit centers, we must be an Edison-inspired agrarian. An Edison-inspired agrarian:

* Embraces a never-ending commitment to learning, questioning, tinkering, questioning, doing, and teaching

* Has a healthy disregard for the norm but a respect for history

* Listens carefully to its customers, channels, strategic partners, and vendors about what the market *really* wants and needs (and what they'll pay for those wants *and* needs)

* Understands how to separate expressions of interest in a new product or service or new feature or capability from the willingness to purchase those things as soon as they become available

* Draws a healthy balance between capitalism and altruism when it comes to innovating to benefit and advance society

* Takes nothing for granted and never becomes complacent when it comes to improving, innovating, and inspiring others to do the same

* Builds teams with a diverse background and skill set but with a unified focus and motivation for excellence

* Overcomes the 12 enemies of innovation success, as shown in Figure 6-2. Each phase of the innovation process faces its share of enemies and the potential for damage, destruction, or derailment. The most common enemies and hurdles are indicated.

Pilots and Pioneers

To be a successful intellectual capital agrarian, you do not need to invent (or reinvent) farming. You may need to uncover new

Figure 6-2. The 12 enemies of successful IP harvest.

Enemy of Budget	Enemy of Time	Enemy of Rose-Colored Glasses
Enemy of Self-Interest	Enemy of Lack of Reputation/Track Record	Enemy of Defensiveness
Enemy of Pessimism	Enemy of Knowledge/Expertise	Enemy of Complacency
Enemy of Politics	Enemy of CYA Syndrome	Enemy of Competition

processes, timetables, and systems to fine-tune your craft. You will need to become skilled in irrigating, plowing, tilling, fertilizing, and nurturing the soil. You'll need to know what the market wants, what price it will pay, and how quickly you need to get your product to it. There will be plenty of room for process, channel, and other forms of incremental innovation along the way. But even those regarded as true pioneers rarely "invented" the product they were selling. Howard Schultz did not invent coffee, but he redefined the value proposition to help us feel good about drinking a $5 Frappucino. Fred Smith did not invent mail delivery, but he did pilot a "hub and spoke" business model that empowered us to embrace a new way of getting things to each other on an overnight basis. Many pioneers fail because they are too far ahead of the demand or product adoptive curve, while others see their first-mover advantage erode over time as bigger players piggyback on the opportunity they have identified and learn from the pioneer's early mistakes. The advantages enjoyed early on in the areas of experience or channel preemption begin to fade as incumbent inertia and technological leapfrogging flood into the pioneer's once empty fields. *In many cases, the first movers are left behind in the dust of those who learned from all of the research undertaken and the mistakes made by the pioneers.* Compare Google's success to Yahoo's or AOL's or RIM's success to that of Motorola or Nokia. Yet, other first movers, such as Netflix, Tiffany, and Nordstrom, seem to thrive, virtually untouched or unaffected by imitators or competitors.

When an intellectual capital agrarian chooses to be a true pioneer in new product development and launch strategy, a variety of metrics must be taken into consideration. These include:

* **Customer Characteristics:** Price sensitivity, consumption patterns, attitudes toward risk, the costs to switch over to

the pioneering product, loyalty to existing alternatives, demographics of target market longevity of demand

* **Product Features:** Clarity of value proposition, real and perceived benefits, limited versus mass market appeal, channel conflict, price for actual or perceived substitutes for pioneering product, life cycle of product category

* **Competitive Environment and Marketplace:** Current economic conditions, expected timing of the "fast followers" new entrants, barriers to entry, availability of comparable "substitutes," competitive and market influencer's expected reaction to new product launch

* **Intellectual Property:** IP strategy selected, strength of brands and distinctiveness, proprietary channels, degrees of patent protection and scope of claims, vulnerability to reverse engineering and copy-cats, success rates for enforcing infringement claims, loyalty to existing ancillary brands, specific covenants in partnering and leveraging relationships

From Pilots to Projects to Profits

Virtually all significant organizational endeavors begin with a spark, an idea, a concept, a proposed solution, a vision, or a new way of thinking that needs to survive certain screens and filters before it matures into a sustainable, durable, and profitable contributor to shareholder value over the long term. There are a number of critical inflection points that these nubile enterprises must overcome before they are ever seen in the marketplace, and these inflection points may vary from company to company and from organization to organization.

Some companies have formalized and centralized R&D departments where all new ideas must be tested and analyzed. Some R&D units are fragmented by division or business functions; some are random and disorganized; some are segregated into an experimental division, team, cross-divisional working group, or "greenhouse"; and some are off-site at a "skunkworks" location. Some companies rely on consultants, partners, and even outsourcing for their new-idea generation and new-venture creation. Other companies, such as Cisco and Oracle, rely on M&A and strategic investments and corporate venture capital discussions to stimulate a pipeline of new ideas.

One very effective program has been the Future Works entrepreneurial arm of Procter & Gamble, which was launched in 2008 to harvest and spin out innovative and creative opportunities that might otherwise be stifled or derailed inside the walls of a global conglomerate. The Future Works initiative has already birthed the launch of Tide dry cleaners, which began franchising in 2009. With 800,000 fans on Facebook and millions of fiercely loyal customers, Future Works analyzed various intellectual capital leveraging opportunities for the Tide brand, and the early initiatives appear to be off to a strong start. Another Future Works initiative is the franchising of a Mr. Clean brand–inspired chain of car washes, and related projects are also under way to better leverage the Pampers, Oil of Olay, and Crest brands. Procter & Gamble is driving shareholder value by not being complacent in the management and harvesting of its more mature and already saturated products and markets and is moving to uncover new opportunities to drive revenues and profits.

Buy-versus-Build Analysis

At what point is it better to buy rather than trying to develop those capabilities from scratch? Factors to consider include:

* Probability of technical success
* Costs (tangible and intangible)
* Speed to market
* Quality/expertise
* Degree of competition in market
* Speed and difficulty/access to building a distribution channel
* Market fragmentation
* Regulation
* Access to financing/cost of reports
* Governance issues
* Customer acquisition costs/timeframe/loyalty
* Supplier acquisition costs/timeframe/loyalty
* R&D capabilities/new-product profile
* Human capital
* IP rights of competitors (as a blocking factor)

Lessons from the Greenhouse

It used to be that farmers grew certain crops only during a specific season suitable for their characteristics. This is no longer true because of farmers' innovative and creative efforts. Agrarians are now able to create the necessary conditions for their plants and vegetables to grow year-round—even when it snows! They build greenhouses that help to keep out harmful hard rains and winds, prevent temperature fluctuations, and allow the natural sunlight to warm up the interior. This helps satisfy market demand for fresh vegetables year-round and brings more cash into farmers' pockets.

Just like crop-driven farmers, intellectual capital agrarians need to think outside the box and create conditions that will enable innovation year-round—even in the most unfavorable winters—and protect prototypical concepts and early-stage ideas from a premature death caused by the harsh conditions of the corporate ecosystem. To qualify for admission into the protection of the greenhouse, the idea or concept should be aligned with corporate objectives, have a nurturing champion, require a reasonable period of time before it can survive outside the protection of the greenhouse, and have an "allowance" on budget allocation assigned for its time in greenhouse tenancy. As we very slowly emerge from the financial recession or perhaps head into a second one, this is an important lesson to keep in mind. Instead of blaming the bad weather or the bad economy or new government regulations, be innovative and build your business's greenhouse. Be an incubator of new ideas, new and improved ways of doing business, or supplying consumers' needs in and out of season.

Actually Flying the Plane

No matter how good flight simulation software may be, most pilots will tell you that there is no real substitute for flying a plane in the sky under a wide variety of weather conditions. Inside companies and organizations, pilot projects are designed to predict the success or failure of a given proposed new product or service, new pricing model, new channel, new store format, new features, new manufacturing processes, new hiring procedures, or new customers or markets (domestic or abroad). But, even the most successful pilots can be in jeopardy when they exit the simulator and take the controls of a real airplane in harsh weather conditions. Intellectual capital agrarians must be committed to ensuring that pilots' projects are as close to "real-life" conditions as possible and that they have been tested with test customers with representative demographics to avoid the appearance of either sandbagging or creating fake hope for the *actual* demand for the new product, service, or roll-out. A restaurant's "soft opening" with test customers who are all friends of the chef and who are saying nice things about the food or service because they don't want to offend her is as effective as the emperor's new clothes are at keeping the emperor warm in the winter. Similarly, positioning a new product in a pilot priced at "loss-leader" levels in the hope that the customer will become hooked and find that she can't live without it thereafter at any price is rarely successful or sustainable.

Intellectual capital agrarians must define what the key elements and inflection points within their company should be before a new offering is formally introduced. The key elements of the featured product or service in the pilot should be clearly identified, streamlined, and priced well before a feasibility study is conducted. Feasibility analysis, proof of concept, beta models, and even test marketing are completely ineffective if the target customer is duped or confused or fails to recognize (or in any way desire) the innovation being introduced. Many companies will test a product or service internally by "running it up the flagpole" with the right internal stakeholders before introducing it externally or will "small-batch" test it in a few markets externally and allow it to succeed or fail relatively quickly with minimal damage to the brand or customer loyalty. This is frequently done in the fashion and hospitality industries. Not only does this contribute to the honesty and integrity of the "smell test," but it also contributes to the overall innovative process.

Some companies misread internal and external market signals that suggest that innovation is desired or necessary. The 1985 launch of New! Coke is an often-cited example of a complete misread of the market and its loyalty to the product that is now known as Coke Classic. Many consumers who objected to the change had not even tasted the new product; their pushback was based on lore, principle, and tradition—which are not to be taken lightly. Coca-Cola learned its lesson and has enjoyed much stronger success with its new varieties, flavors, and sizes; in 2009, it enjoyed tremendous success with its Coke Zero product without cannibalizing on Diet Coke.

Fashion companies, designers, athletes, and celebrities have enjoyed generally strong success when leveraging their brands and reputation into fragrances, shoes, accessories, home textiles and decor, luggage, sunglasses, and apparel. Candy companies such as Hershey's, Mars, and Godiva have extended their brands into other food and beverage lines and multiple price/sizing/packaging varietals. Dole extended its juice brands into fruit salads, frozen fruit bars, and packaged snacks. Ivory extended its trusted soap image into dishwashing liquid, gentle car detergent, and grooming products. Crayola expanded from crayons into markers, pens, paints, and office products. And consumers appear to have readily accepted the extension of Starbucks Coffee into coffee ice cream and ice cream bars, as well.

But line extensions and expansions have also gone awry, as indicated by some of the more unfortunate examples shown in Figure 6-3. Companies have assumed that the loyalty of their customer base extended further than it really did, offering ill-

Figure 6-3. The good, the bad, and the ugly.

The Good	The Bad	The Ugly
(Well done!)	(Nice try!)	(What were they thinking?)
• Caterpillar® (construction machinery) to shoes, watches, and clothing/accessories	• BenGay® (analgesic cream) to aspirin	• Harley Davidson® (motorcycles) to perfumes
• Dunlop® (tires) to shoes, golf balls, tennis racquets, and adhesive	• Country Time® (lemonade) to cider	• Bic® (pens and disposable lighters) to ladies underwear
• Adidas® (sporting gear and shoes) to fragrances and personal hygiene products	• Coors® (beer) to spring water	• Smith and Wesson® (guns) to mountain bikes
• Arm & Hammer® (baking soda) to cleaning products and toothpaste	• Lynx® (body wash) to hair salons	• Cosmopolitan® (magazine) to yogurt (but has succeeded in its bed linen lines)
• IAMS® (pet food) to pet insurance	• LifeSavers® (candy) to soda	• Colgate® (toothpaste) to frozen kitchen entrees
• Starbucks® (coffee) to liqueurs and ice cream	• Campbell® (soups) to spaghetti sauce	• Hooters® (restaurants) to airlines
• Tide to Go® (laundry detergent) to stain removal pen	• Crystal Pepsi (enough said)	• E.T. the Extra Terrestrial® (movie) to action video games
	• Webvan® grocery delivery (never worked)	• Sony® Betamax
	• Kellogg's® cereals to breakfast mates	• Sylvester Stallone (movie star) to chocolate pudding
	• Maxwell House® ground coffee cartoned pre-prepared coffee	• Everlast® (batteries) to cologne and grooming line

conceived and improperly tested brand-extension licensing and partnerships that wound up denigrating goodwill and diluting the integrity and equity of the brand. When Peugeot executives decided to introduce the new Peugeot 404 a year after they had introduced the Peugeot 403 in the U.S. market, instead of yielding increased sales, the move led to a decline in revenue from both models. This was especially shocking because the Peugeot 403 was named by *Road & Track* magazine as one of the seven best-made cars in the world. The problem, according to Al Ries, an account executive working on the launch of the new product, was that, instead of replacing one model with the other, the company showcased the cars next to each other, which made the older model look outdated and the newer model seem too expensive. Peugeot executives misjudged clients' opinion; customers probably would have preferred a single model and viewed the basic model as lacking after seeing the extension. History shows that the world's largest-selling vehicles were often single models with only minor updates on an annual basis, such was Ford's Model T, with more than 15 million sold, and the Volkswagen Beetle, with more than 21 million sold.

Why Do New Product and Service Lines Fail?

Although there are probably hundreds of reasons why newly introduced products and services fail, even when associated with an established and recognized brand, the top six reasons are these:

1. The company misread the scope of the loyalty of its consumers.
2. The company targeted the wrong groups of consumers or assumed that the masses wanted what the classes had or vice versa.
3. The pricing strategy, terms, opportunity costs, or pain to make the switchover were miscalculated or insufficiently researched.
4. A nonoptimal mix of product benefits and features was baked into the packaging.
5. The consumer did not understand the "benefit transfer" of the underlying brand to the extended product or service.
6. The extended product or service did not compete well with other logical choices available to the consumer.

12 Ways to Avoid Pilot Crashes

1. **Assign a diverse pilot team with clear expectations and timetables.** Make sure the pilot team has diversity in background, expertise, and perspectives. Use both internal and external advisers. Set clear deadlines and expectations; do not authorize open-ended fishing expeditions in hopes of finding "a pony among a pile of poop."

2. **Don't overfund or underfund.** Allocate the resources needed to ensure a proper test, but remember that underfunded projects never make it out of the laboratory and overfunded projects lead to waste and "false positives." Set budgets, and hold pilot team members accountable; make sure they have skin in the game.

3. **Focus on markets and communication, not product bells and whistles.** As Edison would say, the mark of a successful invention is a willing and happy buyer, not a product to be put on display at a museum. Commercialization objectives must trump development or dreams of design awards.

4. **Garner internal support and enthusiasm at the highest level.** Pilots need momentum and physical support to survive. Engage leadership early on, and lobby across divisional lines to gain internal support and build enthusiasm.

5. **Open the doors to collaboration and communication with customers and channel partners.** It is often asked, "Will the dog eat the dog food?" We can test, speculate, and pontificate all day long about the likely success of a given product or service, but, at the end of the day, if the channel partners are not excited to sell the product and customers are not excited to buy the product, it will surely fail. Seek input for improvement, positioning, and pricing from all key stakeholders in the process.

6. **Close the gaps.** Pilot project planning must be crisp, with all key steps identified and executed. Accountability at each step is critical. Too much "wiggle room" or "white space" between key steps leads to waste, haste, and unnecessary delay, and the

(continues)

135

failure to anticipate problems leaves the crops to rot on the vine while everyone is debating how or when to pick them.

7. **Integrate and include.** Pilot project success must be an integrated and inclusive undertaking, free from silos, turf wars, and internal or external politics. Excluding key constituencies or key players in the process is a fatal mistake, but knowing exactly *when* to include certain constituencies (especially those likely to kill a project) is both an art and science and is company ecosystem-specific. Empower initial working teams with all of the access to information that they need to succeed or fail. All pieces of the pilot project must be woven together with the intricacy of a multiparty quilting club working on a large quilt. The only way to ensure that all puzzle pieces fit together and that "buy-in" will occur at all critical levels and subject areas is to involve the right players at the right time and in the right place in the right mindset.

8. **Keep your head out of the sand.** Charles Darwin wrote, "It is not the strongest of species that survive, or the most intelligent, but the one most responsive to change." A pilot project team that is too set in its ways and unable to evolve will die. In some cases, teams become so set in their ways that they can't possibly imagine that there is an alternative path to creating the innovation.

9. **Evaluate risks.** New projects and pilots bring new levels of risk, which must be understood and managed. Risks should be calculated and measured from a liability perspective, a brand integrity perspective, a customer loyalty perspective, and a product replacement perspective; they must also be looked at in terms of their impact on other divisions. Metrics must reveal actual, perceived, and inherent risks. For more on this topic, see Craig R. Davis, "Calculated Risk: A Framework for Evaluating Product Development," *MIT Sloan Review* (Summer 2002).

10. **Develop a healthy project management culture.** To be truthful, some companies are good at managing pilot projects (or any project at all), and some are not. The assembly of the right team, the clear definition of expectations of rewards, the level of time commitment (measured against other responsibilities), the right mix of skill sets, access to resources, and

empowerment to fail without consequence are all critical success factors. The bottom line is that if team members are too busy in their "day jobs" to contribute to pilot projects involving innovation initiatives, then no seeds will be planted, no crops will grow, and no new innovation will be harvested. Intellectual capital agrarians cannot be an "I'll get to it when I get it" level of commitment; you need to conduct yourself like the parent, not the babysitter.

11. **Mistake early and mistake often.** In the creative and product development process, all the best learning comes from the biggest mistakes. Put them as early in the alpha/beta/prototype stage as you can; they get harder and more expensive to fix as the process gets further along.

12. **Value both the silver and the gold.** Remember the old children's song "Make new friends, but keep the old/One is silver and the other's gold"? The same holds true for intellectual capital agrarianism. Reliable, profit-generating "cash cows" should not be put to slaughter prematurely, but do not allow their productivity and predictable returns to be an excuse to delay the raising of new, young calves. Intellectual capital agrarians need to strike a balance between making sure that the crops in the field have been sufficiently harvested and the land refertilized before new crops are planted or new "green fields" are explored. As experienced fishermen always say, "Don't leave fish to find fish—but you'll never know what may be waiting on the other side of the lake if you stay stuck in the same hole."

Some Lessons from Companies That Are Particularly Strong at New Product Development

Procter & Gamble (P&G), which made innovation one of its five core strengths, has been able to successfully introduce many new products to the market. In 2009 alone, P&G had 5 of the top 10 new product launches in the United States and 10 of the top 25. In addition to budgeting for high levels of R&D funding (the company invests twice as much on average as its leading competitors), P&G transformed its traditional in-house R&D process into an open-source innovation strategy known as "connect-and-develop."

This method is designed to harvest the collective intellectual power of the world by leveraging external sources' (even competitors') innovation assets—products, intellectual property, and people—to drive its innovation. The strategy is not to replace the capabilities of P&G's 7,500 researchers and support staff but to better leverage them. To this end, P&G created new job classifications such as "technology entrepreneurs" (TEs), who act as scouts, looking for the latest breakthroughs from places such as university labs. P&G is thus able to identify promising ideas throughout the world and apply its own R&D, manufacturing, marketing, and purchasing capabilities to them to create better and cheaper products faster. In 2006, more than 35 percent of P&G new products included elements that originated from outside P&G. In the same year, 45 percent of P&G's product development initiatives had key elements that were discovered externally. The connect-and-develop innovation model helped double P&G's internal innovation success rate, while lowering its cost of innovation.

IBM has also reached out beyond its lab for new product development ideas. IBM, which holds more patents (30,000 to date) than any other U.S.-based technology business, uses "collaboratories" to innovate. These "collaboratories" are small, regional joint ventures with universities, foreign governments, or commercial partners. They are designed to tap into local skills, funding, and sales channels in order to get new technology quickly into the marketplace. IBM is also increasingly collaborating with customers in order to create new products that satisfy market demand. For example, IBM is working with a prominent candy company to apply a prototype of a Web analysis tool, called Business Insights Workbench (BIW), to find hidden patterns and meaning in structured and unstructured data that will help predict whether a particular brand of chocolate will be bought in emerging markets. By working directly with customers, IBM is able to tap into customers' intellectual capacities and create products that are in demand.

Beyond successfully leveraging outside intellectual capital and harvesting in-house human capital, IBM is one of the world's most innovative companies because of its ability to repeatedly reinvent itself as the technology paradigms shift. IBM utilizes changed circumstances as opportunities for new products. IBM has come far from developing the first PC and selling hardware, re-creating itself as a global technology consultant. For example, it has collaborated with a Toronto hospital to help doctors monitor minute changes in the health of premature babies. By being flexible and embracing changes, IBM has been able to bring many new products to the market.

The concept of reaching out beyond the company's walls for ideas has been implemented at Nokia, as well. Nokia Pilots is a program that helps get Nokia users involved in the company's creative development process by allowing users to share their ideas and suggest improvements that can be put into action. Anybody interested can register and become a Nokia Pilot candidate, and those who are selected advise the research and development and sales and marketing teams without monetary compensation. Nokia Pilots and other similar programs are a great way to gain access to ideas while incurring minimal expenses.

Yet another lesson comes from Southwest Airlines, one of the few airlines to remain profitable after 9/11. Southwest Airlines was able to innovate because it involved people of diverse backgrounds and skills in its planning/strategic/research committees and managed its fuel cost supply chain very effectively. The company gathered people from its in-flight, ground, maintenance, and dispatch operations to brainstorm ideas to address possible changes to aircraft operations. Because of the diverse outlooks and naïve perspectives of the varied committee members, the management was forced to reevaluate some of the business premises it had taken for granted and to implement sweeping operational changes. The result was increased efficiency and profits. Fostering diversity across all levels of a company's human capital leads to increased creativity and innovation.

A Four-Step Filtering Tool

In addition to all of the best practices, insights, and observations presented up to this point in the chapter, it is also useful to develop a screening tool that weighs key variables and helps an intellectual capital agrarian determine what is wheat and what must be discarded or delayed as either chaff or wheat not ready to be picked. In the text that follows and in Figures 6-4 through 6-7, I have included a four-step tool developed by my Smith School of Business colleague Oliver Schlake for screening new ideas and concepts.

Step 1. Develop a list of screening criteria customized to your company's goals and objectives.

Here is a list of 12 representative criteria used by Professor Schlake:

1. **Criteria for attractiveness scoring (strategic fit):** R&T program fit with business or corporate strategy
2. **Probability of technical success:** Probability of overcoming technical hurdles within five years, determined by assessment of program complexity, company technology skill base, available technical knowledge
3. **Probability of commercial success:** Probability of market adoption with attractive industry dynamics, determined by projections of market need, company's marketing capabilities, and company's application and development skills
4. **Potential for R&T spin-offs:** Extent to which R&T program serves as a platform for growth; ranges from "one of a kind" to "opens up new technical and commercial fields"
5. **Proprietary nature:** Measures company's ability to maintain a unique technical position as a result of a successful project
6. **Reward (ROCE/incremental profits):** Assessment of projected return on capital employed within three years of first commercial use and incremental profit impact
7. **R&T cost to commercialize:** Cumulative R&T costs from today into the future expected until commercial operations begin; measurement of level of R&T investment required, including R&T capital expenditures such as pilot plants
8. **Time to first commercial sales/use:** Number of years until the results of the program are actually used in producing a commercial product
9. **Environment, health, and safety impact:** Perceived impact on high-profile issues (e.g., a recycling theme may have positive impact)
10. **Platform for expansion:** Level of program synergy with other businesses in the company; ranges from "one of a kind" to "affects multiple businesses"
11. **Incremental capital at risk (early user, new technology):** Capital investment (not including plants) required to commercialize the program
12. **Competitive position postproject (market position):** Impact of the project on the company's market position within the industry; the Q in the Q/C ratio

Step 2. *Score the proposed innovation project first according to its strategic fit with the organization's overall goals and objectives, as shown in Figure 6-4.*

Figure 6-4. Strategic fit—top criteria.

Definition:

R&T Program fit with business or corporate strategy.

Detailed Scale:	Overall Scale: 1 2 3 (Low)	4 5 6 7 (Medium)	8 9 10 (High)	
Clear strategic plan + technology focus	2	5	7	10
Somewhat clear, frequent changes	2	4	6	8
Limited to short-term goals only	1	2	4	6
Unclear direction	1	1	2	3
	None	Modest	Good	Excellent
	Degree of Program Alignment			

Step 3. Develop a project attractiveness score sheet based on the weighting of other relevant variables, as shown in Figure 6-5.

Figure 6-5. Project attractiveness score sheet

Rating:				Score 1		Score 2		Score 3	
10 — 100% fulfillment; 5 — 50% fulfillment; 1 — marginal fulfillment; 0 — no score; Total score = sum of all ratings x weight									
Criteria									
1. Strategic fit	10		8	=80	7	70	6	60	
2. R&T cost to commercialize	2		9	=18	7	14	9	18	
3. Competitive position post project	8		5	=40	3	24	5	40	
4. Probability of commercial success	8		9	=72	6	48	10	80	
5. Environment, health, and safety impacts	7		3	=21	4	28	3	21	
6. Platform for expansion	7		8	=56	6	42	5	35	
7. Proprietary nature	5		8	=40	9	45	10	50	
8. Reward (ROCE + incremental profits)	10		8	=80	9	90	9	90	
Total attractiveness score (1000 max.)				407		361		394	

Step 4: Determine allocation of resources, staffing, timetable, and priorities, based on the scoring in Figure 6-5 and guided by new variables such as attractiveness, portfolio balance determination, reward, market and competitive conditions, and customer needs, as shown in Figures 6-6 and 6-7.

Figure 6-6. Strategic purpose of innovation.

A Survival
Enables the company to survive [where it should survive]
Provide capability only where not available elsewhere

D Reposition the company
Reposition the company for sustainable leadership
Concentrate on major unique new products and processes

B Technical support
Provide technical support to manufacturing & customers not available in operations or economically outside

E Build knowledge
Most companies have zero, may contract at universities or institutes

C Sustainable Leadership
Make improvements to maintain or develop sustainable leadership
Concentrate on programs to position company as a leading competitor

F Develop non-leadership
Make improvements to maintain or develop non-leadership business
Provide capability only when not available elsewhere

Figure 6-7. Portfolio balance determination.

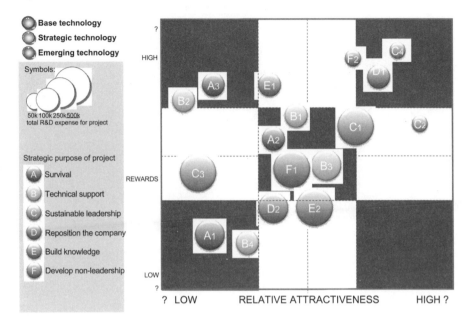

CHAPTER 7

Bringing the Crops to the Marketplace: An Overview of Strategic Alternatives

It is not the strongest of species that survive, nor the most intelligent, but the ones most responsive to change.

—CHARLES DARWIN

We really have two basic choices in life—we can either share knowledge or keep it to ourselves. When we decide to keep it to ourselves, we have decided that this knowledge, such as the secret formula for Coke, provides us with a competitive edge in the marketplace, the release of which would cause significant damage to our shareholders. The law gives us choices and strategies for protecting our intellectual properties to the exclusion of the rights of others. When we choose to share the knowledge, we have decided that the sum is greater than the whole of the parts, that, whether via licensing, joint ventures, consortiums, franchising, or some other device, our knowledge will be *more* valuable if we allow others to access it under some form of intellectual capital agrarian harvesting strategy and structure.

Once the intellectual capital has been planted, nurtured, grown, and harvested, various growth structures must be evaluated in order to develop an Agrarian Leveraging Plan (ALP) for bringing the crops to the marketplace. The ALP will guide us like a road map as we move along the highway of maximization of shareholder value and explanation of new opportunity.

The ALP is your road map as to what to do with your intellectual asset crops once they have been harvested to drive and maximize shareholder value. It details a pathway for squeezing the most juice from every orange, as well as for harvesting the pulp and the rind.

Intellectual capital agrarians, like their farmer brethren, not only are interested in driving profitable income streams but are also focused on avoiding waste and inefficiency, especially in a society guided by environment, recycling, and sustainability. For decades, farmers have recycled food waste into compost, fed animals with food excess, used cattle manure as a source of energy, utilized reservoirs and aqueduct systems to catch and store atmospheric water, salvaged metal and reused it for furniture, building, or fence construction. Today, the trend to preserve, reuse, and recycle for economic and efficiency reasons continues on many family farms and is being reintroduced in larger commercial farms. Stonyfield Farm, a dairy farm from New Hampshire, is one such example. Recently, it saved more than $70,000 annually by retrofitting its manufacturing process, installing energy-efficient lighting fixtures and hot-water heat-recovery systems to capture "waste" heat, and recycling all cardboard, paper, aluminum, and many plastics.

Finally, corporate America is following suit. After installing a treatment facility in 2006, General Mills has been using food-processing waste water for cooling and dusting purposes. Today, as much as half of the plant's water can now be treated, restored, and reused, trimming the plant's overall water consumption by an average of 46 percent—or about 5.3 million gallons per month—and saving the company about $840,000 per year.

In 2010, General Mills announced that the "holes" in Cheerios are now being used as a source of energy to fuel its plants. Bakers at Dunkin' Donuts years ago were tired of the waste and cost of discarding the dough that made up the donut holes and began selling them as a stand-alone baked good, which remains very popular today as a bite-sized donut. Where are the "holes" in your business? Where are the areas that typically go to waste that can be harvested into valuable and revenue-generating/cost-saving assets? Customers, stock markets, and the environment are ready to reward those who avoid waste and can transform it into something useful—a type of strategic fertilizer that now not only has its own value-enhancing powers but also spurns and harvests new products, services, and efficiencies.

I once had the pleasure of sitting in on a presentation at WeConnect (www.weconnect.org) from the Self-Employed Women's Association (SEWA), based in India, which had piloted a project that collected paper trash from the crowded streets of Bangalore, Delhi, and 12 districts in Gujarat and transformed them into beautiful recycled paper, pottery, shopping bags, presentation binders, jewelry, and other gifts. To date, there are more than 32,000 women workers who are waste-paper pickers, and the numbers rise each month. Making the most out of your trash and the waste of others is not only an intellectual capital agrarian best practice; it's also simply the right thing to do for future generations.

To properly harvest and leverage your intellectual assets, you need to develop an ALP, which will help your company to map out where you are, what you have achieved, and where you are going and will explain why you plan to head in that direction. Effective business and strategic planning is *critical* to an intellectual capital agrarian's long-term success and its ability to harvest its intellectual assets and grow successfully.

Four Critical Steps in Building an Agrarian Leveraging Plan

There are four critical steps in developing an agrarian leveraging plan, which are detailed in the pages that follow, The failure to develop a harvesting plan will ensure that crops are watered or rot on the vine. In this section, we ensure that all crops of value reach the intended marketplace in a timely and efficient manner.

* **Step 1: Perform a fish-or-fowl analysis.** Which type of innovation asset are we leveraging? How will the type of innovation asset affect our analysis and planning?

* **Step 2: Perform a SWOT analysis.** What are the strengths, weaknesses, opportunities, and threats that may influence this new product or service?

* **Step 3: Draft the agrarian leveraging plan.** Will we roll out this new product or service via existing channels or establish new pathways to the marketplace? Will we go it alone or pursue interdependent, third-party relationships? Or strategic partnerships? Or multiparty structures?

* **Step 4: Complete a sensitivity analysis.** The implementation of the ALP must be carefully monitored, adjusted, updated, and redefined on the basis of the successes and the failures encountered along the way. The "what ifs" must be addressed from both an upside and a downside perspective. Unexpected changes in market conditions, demand patterns, and competitive analysis all must be factored in to the evolution of the ALP.

Step 1: Perform a Fish-or-Fowl Analysis

As we saw in Chapter 6, the type of innovation often dictates the corresponding strategic plan that must be developed for the innovation to be properly harvested. It can broaden or narrow the range of options according to the degree of incrementalization, the likely rate of adoption, the type of intellectual property protection available, the impact on current channels, the availability of financial resources, the availability of human capital and expertise, and scalability and internal levels of champions.

Figure 7-1 offers an overview of the degrees and types of innovation available.

As mentioned earlier in this book, breakthrough innovation is rare, and we may experience only a few of these in each of our lifetimes. For the baby boomer generation, breakthroughs in communication (cellular phones, the Internet, smart phones) and in medicine (biotechnology, laser surgery, MRIs, DNA research) have changed our lives, as well as the ways in which we interact with others. But the bulk of innovation is incremental in nature and is focused at the consumer level or on making existing things better, easier to use, lower in cost, more pleasant to experience, or more meaningful to us. Behind the scenes, business-model and process innovations create competitive advantage and drive

Figure 7-1. Degrees and types of innovation.

(How novel or unique is the innovation when benchmarked against what is currently available?)

Breakthrough/New to the World (The Wheel, Fire, Cement, Measurement, Language, Fuel)		

Major Game Changers (Internet, DNA technology, Liquid Crystal Displays, Magnetic Resonance Imaging, Pacemaker, Insulin, Laser Surgery, etc.)	**Quality of Life Influencers** (Printing Press, Automobiles, Air Travel, Radio, Television, Microwave Oven, Personal Computers/Laptops, Cellular Phone Technology, PDAs, etc.)	**Paradigm Shift In Process** (Production, Distribution and Administrative Approaches to Lower Costs, Improve Quality, Speed Delivery, or Enhance Customer Experience!) Ex's: GEICO, Federal Express

Customer Service Innovation (Nordstrom, Southwest Airlines, Starbucks, Google)	**Business Model Innovation** (e-Bay, Priceline, CNN, Car Max, Schwab, Remax, etc.)	**New Applications for Existing Product or Source Lines**	**Modifications/Improvement to Existing Products** (Longlasting Light-Bulbs, Diet Soda, Lowfat Snacks, etc.)

View to a Market McDonald's in China, Honda/Toyota's entry into U.S., etc.)	**New Product Lines For Existing Company** (Organic/Partnered/M&A) (Wendy's/Tim Houston's)	**Additions to Existing Product or Service Lines** (iPad joins iPod)	**Product Enhancements Revisions/Additions** (iPod colors, sizes, and accessories)

Repositioning/Rebranding	Cost Reduction/ Distribution Efficiency	**Incremental Improvement to Features/Ease of Use** (Remote Control, Navigation Tools	Incremental Branding Strategies to Relatively Homogenous Products (Ex: Just Do It (Nike), Perrier/Evian (Water)

shareholder value in the areas of production techniques, distribution channels, marketing and branding strategies, supply chain and purchasing systems, compensation and management strategies, cost containment, administrative systems, and operational logistics. Process innovations may not make headline news, but companies strive to improve customer loyalty and mindshare every day by improving retail design, financing methods, service delivery systems, health and safety features, maintenance and repair support, procurement techniques, customer service and training systems, sales commission structures, and in-store merchandising, all of which influence our retail and online shopping and services consumption experiences.

A company's commitment to innovation is admirable, but the harder decisions then must be made as to *which* types of innovation will benefit from a commitment of the company's time, people, and resources and how those commitments will align with the real wants and needs of the company's current and target customers. Companies must be careful not to "out-innovate" or "mis-innovate," which alienates customers instead of strengthening ties with them. It is also critical to understand which elements drive customer satisfaction—there is the often-cited example of the chef who kept tinkering with his menu to build a loyal base of regular customers, when the main thing that would have brought them back was cleaner bathrooms.

So let's look at a hypothetical example to move toward the process of building the ALP. McDonald's Corporation, building on the huge success of its Chipotle spin-off, its new healthy menu, and its successful roll-out of an upscale but affordable coffee line, decides to expand into the fast-food Chinese cuisine business. This new product line could be pursued in a variety of ways, including:

* Introducing a few new menu items at *existing* company-owned or franchised locations (likely on a initial test-pilot basis)

* Establishing a stand-alone line of company-owned or franchised McSoy business formats (which may or not be offered to existing franchisees in good standing)

* "Licensing in" a series of branded ingredients or recipes from an already established name in the Chinese food sector (McSoy features La Choy products) in a license (or joint venture) with Con Agra

* Acquiring an existing Chinese food chain such as Panda as a "foundation for future growth and perhaps even a spin-off (as it did with Chipotle)

* Entering into a joint venture with an existing chain or finding a smaller chain with high growth potential (once McDonald's adds its expertise)

* Forming a marketing or operational cooperative or serving as a regional food and supply commissary resource center for existing (or to be converted to McSoy) Chinese restaurants

Clearly, McDonald's has an opportunity to harvest its intellectual assets (its system, brand, processes, manuals, purchasing power, relationships, hospitality expertise, goodwill) into a new opportunity, but the type and degree of innovation will influence the strategy (or strategies—they are not necessarily mutually exclusive) that will be selected for implementation.

Step 2: Perform a SWOT Analysis

Although a detailed discussion of how to conduct a SWOT (strengths, weaknesses, opportunities, threats) analysis is beyond the scope of this book, let's look at some variables in the analysis of our hypothetical example.

Strengths

* Domestic and global expertise in fast-food operations
* Franchisees and customers hungry for new opportunities and driving choices

Weaknesses

* Lack of specific knowledge or expertise in Chinese food segment
* Risk of channel conflict with existing franchisees
* May not offer global expansion opportunities beyond United States
* Still unclear whether consumer will embrace this line extension or whether it is consistent with core values, strengths, and mission (e.g., kid's meals, family fun, parties, Ronald McDonald)

Opportunities

* Leverage the systems and expertise of McDonald's training and field support

* Continue to expand the "family" into healthier food lines

* Capture a stronger "dinner" crowd with Chinese offerings

* Cross-sell McDonald's and Chipotle brands to McSoy customers and develop co-branded units

Threats

* Damage and dilution to McDonald's brand if new product/ service fails

* Robust competition in this segment presented already by Panda, Pei Wei Asian Diner (owned by P. F. Chang's), Manchu Wok, and The Great Wall

* Food costs, labor costs, quality control, store build-out (costs may dictate a business model entirely different from those of Chipotle and McDonald's)

Mapping Out Your Ecosystem

Ecosystem mapping is a key strategic prerequisite to building an ALP and should be performed as an integral part of the SWOT analysis. Every company, regardless of size or industry, operates within one (or more) ecosystems.

To effectively map out your company's ecosystem, it is critical to ask the following questions:

* Where do we fit in?

* Who are the key players and stakeholders? Who makes the rules and sets the standards? Who (or what) has the power to change them? What are their key issues, concerns, and needs? Who are the decision makers? The market influencers?

* What are the dynamics? The pecking order? The politics? The hurdles and barriers?

* Have we conducted a meaningful competitive analysis?

* Where are the windows of opportunity? What relationships are penetrable, and which ones are opaque?

* What are the key associations, clubs, and professional societies that also exist in the ecosystem (often as a subsystem or parallel system)? What groups *ought* there to be?

* How well is the ecosystem functioning? What variable or events could upset or derail the ecosystem? What would be needed to put it back on track?

Step 3: Draft the ALP

After the SWOT analysis is complete, it's time to prepare the ALP. The most relevant information for the plan may be ambiguous in nature and is likely to change about as often as the weather—but, hey, if the real agrarians can adjust to shifting weather patterns, so can you! No one source can predict where the market is heading and whether McSoy will be the next Chipotle or the next ArchBurger, which died a quick and sudden death. The intellectual capital agrarian must keep his or her eyes wide open and his or her ears close to the ground in building the ALP, carefully monitoring driving market forces, early warning signs, and key metrics and indicators to determine the how, when, and why elements of the plan. Every journey into the unknown starts with a road map and a game plan and then is adjusted accordingly as the unexpected upside and downside surprises of human nature and the marketplace present themselves. By focusing on innovation in an adjacent (or what *appears* to be an adjacent) marketplace, as McDonald's is doing with McSoy, you can mitigate the risk of failure, but there is no way to eliminate the risk.

There's no one single proper format for drafting an ALP.

Rather, the intellectual capital agrarian's properly drafted plan should tell a story, make an argument, and conservatively predict the future. All companies have different stories to tell, different arguments to make, and different futures to predict.

Business-growth planning is the process of setting goals, explaining the objectives, and then mapping out a plan to achieve these goals and objectives. A well-written ALP maps out the best intellectual capital leveraging path and strategy, as well as the rationale for the selection of one strategy over alternatives. In essence, a business-growth plan is the articulation and explanation of *why* your chosen strategy makes sense, *what* resources you will need to implement the growth strategy, *who* will be on the team that will have the vision and leadership to execute the growth strategy, and *what* path the team will follow to get there. It also answers the following questions:

* Who are you?
* What do you do?
* What is your business model? (How do you make money? Who is your customer? What problem do you solve? How do you solve the problem better, faster, or cheaper than other available solutions?)
* How do your customers pay you?
* How loyal are they?
* How should you grow?
* Why is this strategy better than others that may be available?
* What do you need to implement the growth strategy selected?
* How crowded is the market?
* What channels (and at what costs) will you use to sell the customer *your* product or service? Why are these the best channels?
* What market research have you done to be sure that anyone *wants* to buy this product or service at this price—or at all?

* Does your company truly modify the way business is being done in your industry (as a change agent), or is this more of a fad or a trend?

Nobody has a crystal ball to predict what will work and what won't—neither the savviest investor nor the most veteran entrepreneur. The better the analysis, the better the chances that most of the goals set forth in the business-growth plan will be achieved. Harvesting intellectual capital is a marathon, not a sprint.

An Outline of the ALP

A well-written intellectual capital harvesting plan doesn't oversell the good, undersell the bad, or ignore the ugly! It is essentially a plan to manage the risks and challenges involved in implementing a new growth strategy based on the assets being developed. Intellectual capital harvesting plans should acknowledge that growth and success are moving targets by anticipating as many future events or circumstances that will affect the company's objectives. What follows is an outline of the ALP.

I. **Executive Summary**
   A. Brief history of your company
   B. Overview of current products and services and the new business lines that are proposed (is there alignment?)
   C. Background of the management team to staff the new initiatives (summary)
   D. Mission statement (Why are you in this business, and why do you want to be in this *new* business?)
   E. Summary of your company's financial performance to date (where applicable)
   F. Key features of your market and the new adjacent market

II. Company Overview

A. Organizational and management structure

B. Operational and management policies

C. Description of products and services (both current and anticipated)

D. Overview of trends in the industry and marketplace in which you compete (or plan to compete)

E. Key strengths and weaknesses of your company

III. Growth Strategy Analysis

A. How and why did you adopt this growth strategy?

B. What hurdles and risks might you encounter in the implementation of this strategy?

C. What resources will you need to implement this strategy?

D. What market entry strategies are being considered, and why?

E. What new relationship will you have to establish? How will existing stakeholders be affected?

IV. Market Analysis

A. Extended description of the markets in which you compete (e.g., size, trends, growth) and in which you *will* compete

B. Analysis of key competitors and likely future competitors (and how your business model and growth strategy will change or evolve to face the new competitors)

C. Description and analysis of key customers and clients (current and anticipated)

D. Market research supporting current and anticipated product lines

E. Analysis of barriers to entry and your sustainable competitive advantage

V. Marketing and Advertising Strategy

A. Strategies for reaching current and anticipated customers/clients (and expanding scope of existing relationship and loyalties)

B. Pricing policies and strategies

C. Advertising and public relations plans and strategies

D. Discussion of potential market partners and strategic alliances

VI. Financial Plan and Strategies

A. Current financial performance and condition (attach recent income statements and balance sheets)

B. Summary of projected performance for next three to five years (based on new product or service line)

C. Sources of capital to fund roll-out (internal/external)

D. Extended discussion of anticipated allocation of proceeds and parallel budgets

VII. Suggested Exhibits and Attachments

A. Résumés of key members of your management team

B. Organizational chart

C. Timetables for completion of goals and objectives

D. Copies of key documents and contracts

E. Copies of recent media coverage

F. Pictures of key products or advertising materials for services offered

G. List of customer and professional references

Spreading the Fertilizer

As noted in section VI.C. of the ALP draft outline, new product or service innovation must identify the internal and external sources of capital that will serve as the fuel and the fertilizer to harvest these intellectual capital crops and bring them to the marketplace. (See my book *Raising Capital* for more information on capital formation strategies.)

For smaller companies, leaders typically need to either bootstrap or raise external debt or equity capital to foster innovation projects.

But, for global companies, the situation may be different. The fall of 2010 was a fascinating inflection point—as the recession waned, earnings were improving and cash was being stockpiled. By mid-December 2010, nonfinancial companies had accumulated more than $2 trillion in cash, which they kept essentially sitting on the sidelines waiting for deployment.

There are two universal truths—that cash cannot remain idle indefinitely and that cash is not capable of earning the same returns on shareholder equity as it can when deployed strategically, especially in record-low interest rate environments. And U.S. citizens seem to be following the same pattern, with $9 trillion as of December 2010 in savings accounts, certificates of deposit, and money market funds paying almost nothing (less than 2 percent). As a matter of strategy and intellectual capital agrarianism, this cash should be allocated to increased R&D investments, strategic internal/external venture capital–style investments, the building of stronger channels, expansion into overseas markets, expansion of product and service lines, the establishment of David/Goliath partnerships, and new M&A activity and other intellectual capital harvesting and growth strategy designed to maximize shareholder value. For example, Cisco, Microsoft, and Apple each had in excess of $25 to $30 billion in cash on their balance sheets with no apparent plans to declare a special dividend. This cash needs to be put to work to drive shareholder value.

Step 4: Complete a Sensitivity Analysis

As previously discussed, a well-drafted ALP becomes the road map for implementing the company's intellectual capital harvesting strategies by outlining what steps need to be taken, when, how, and by whom. It focuses on key components such as resources, branding, market partners, and distribution channels. *But it must also deal with the inevitable contingencies.* The intellectual capital agrarian's ability to identify specific tasks and translate them into a specific schedule is limited by ever-changing capital markets and customer demand patterns, the entry of new competitors, and general market conditions. The ALP must deal with the "what ifs?" and reflect changing business models. For example, if the success of the ALP relies upon your company's products being faster, cheaper, more reliable, or better able to solve complicated problems than those offered by your competitors, how does the strategy change when your competitor introduces a product that is better, faster, and cheaper than yours? What if the customer is slow to adopt or even recognize the benefits of your new product or service? These are the challenges that high-technology companies face constantly and are the kinds of problems that sensitivity analysis in the ALP seeks to address.

Sensitivity analysis is a tool for looking at a wide range of variables and assumptions in the ALP to determine the impact on the company and the viability of the plan if and when these planning assumptions change—which they invariably and inevitably will.

A sensitivity analysis might raise the following kinds of questions:

* Will our ALP still be viable if 20 percent of the target customers that we assume will adopt this new product do not? 30 percent? 40 percent?

* What impact will it have on our ALP if two of the key *potential* competitors we have identified become actual competitors?

* What impact will it have on our ALP if we can't attract new employees or strategic partners that we have identified as critical to implementation?

* What if we can't raise the equity capital we need to implement the strategy? What if we have to give up more ownership and control than we had anticipated to raise the capital?

* If we plan to borrow money to implement the strategy, what impact will higher interest rates have on the economics of the strategy? If our customers will need to borrow to buy our products and services, what impact will higher rates have on these buying decisions?

* What if the market rejects the pricing structure that underlies the introduction of the new product or service? What if we have to offer deeper discounts to motivate customers to make the switch? What impact will this have on our margins?

The bottom line is that overly optimistic or weakly researched assumptions in your ALP can and will come back to haunt you. And, even if you are conservative in your assumptions and conduct adequate research, there are still many variables that can and will change that will have an impact on your ALP and your company. Sensitivity analysis seeks to *anticipate* the changes in these variables so that you are not caught by surprise.

Variables Likely to Affect the Success or Failure of Implementation of the ALP

No matter how well you plan, things can and will change. Hundreds of variables will go into the development of your ALP, which means that thousands of things could go wrong (or right) that will affect your company's actual-to-plan performance. The actual growth results may vary depending on a wide variety of factors, including:

* Demand for your products and services

* Actions taken by your competitors, including new product introductions and enhancements

* Ability to scale your network and operations to support large numbers of customers, suppliers, and transactions

* Ability to develop, introduce, and market new products and enhancements to your existing products on a timely basis

* Changes in your pricing policies and business model or those of your competitors

* Integration of your recent acquisitions and any future acquisitions

* Ability to expand your sales and marketing operations, including the hiring of additional sales personnel

* Size and timing of sales of your products and services, including the recognition of a significant portion of your sales at the end of the quarter

* Success in maintaining and enhancing existing relationships and developing new relationships with strategic partners, including systems integrators and other implementation partners

* Compensation policies that compensate sales personnel on the basis of whether they achieve annual quotas

* Ability to control costs

* Technological changes in your markets

* Deferrals of customer orders in anticipation of product enhancements or new products

* Customer budget cycles and changes in these budget cycles

* General economic factors, including an economic slowdown or recession

Best Practices in the Development of the ALP

Effective intellectual harvesting planning is not an easy process, and the chapters that follow give your company some of the tools and strategies that it will need to remain viable and competitive. Having worked with hundreds of companies of all sizes and in many different industries over the years to develop business growth strategies, I have pulled together some tips, thoughts, and best practices that should govern your planning process. These are the most important:

* **Have the right mix of talent to develop and maintain your plan.** The wrong planning team will yield the wrong planning decisions, leading the company down a path of disaster.

* **Think long term but act short term.** Be ready to modify the plan to respond to changes in market conditions, but without taking your eye off the long-term goals.

* **Effective business growth planning is a continuing process, not a stand-alone task.**

* **Don't buy into the mantra that planning is a thing of the past.** There are some who believe that market conditions are too dynamic and uncertain to make long-term business growth–oriented strategic planning possible—*this is simply not true!* In fact, fast-moving business conditions make the need for strategic planning that much more important, provided that the plan does not sit on a shelf but rather is monitored and modified as conditions may warrant.

* **Invest in systems that will gather competitive intelligence.** Information rules. If you don't have good data on the trends affecting your competitors and customers, you are dead in the water. The data gathered become a key component of your ALP and the trigger point for changes to the plan or strategy selected.

* **Protect your key assets.** You can develop ALPs until you are blue in the face, but, if the success of your strategy

depends on your ability to keep and leverage your key intangible assets, then you must take the time to protect your intellectual property (see Chapter 5) and to reward and motivate your employees (Chapters 2 and 3).

* **Be sure to connect the dots.** A well-drafted ALP understands and anticipates how all of the market forces and players fit together, taking into account social, environmental, political, and economic influences and figuring out how these factors come together to affect your growth plans. The ability to view things at 30,000 feet and to see the dynamics of your markets at these levels are key to effective growth planning. And, because these market conditions are never static and the relationships that connect the dots constantly change, you need to keep climbing the mountain to look down on the valley.

* **Build an organization that has a deeply rooted commitment to growth.** The commitment must begin with the company's leader or founder, whose mission and passion become contagious and encourage everyone in the company to work toward meeting business growth objectives. To achieve this, the company's leadership must clearly communicate and reinforce the growth plans, objectives, and strategies; reward those who contribute to the achievement of these goals; and monitor the company's progress, changing its course and direction as necessary. If the course does need to change, these shifts in direction must be regularly shared with the company's employees, together with an explanation for the need for the change. Employees at all levels will resent a change in direction if they don't understand it and if they are not told how or why their positions and tasks must change to meet these new challenges.

* **Don't be afraid to measure and monitor performance.** It is critical that you develop an objective set of metrics for

each key area of the ALP that can be continuously monitored and periodically measured against your key goals. The metrics may include sales, profitability, the number of new customer relationships added, the growth market partners, the number of new employees, customer satisfaction, the level of employee turnover, inventory cycles, the number of new offices opened, warranty returns, or even the number of new rounds of capital raised at favorable valuation rates. Regardless of the specific metric(s) selected, the growing company must build systems to track and measure these performance indicators and have the expertise in place to understand, analyze, and properly react to the data once they have been reported.

* **Develop high-quality products and services.** As veteran entrepreneurs and professional advisers will always tell you, an ALP will be completely ineffective if the "dogs will not eat the dog food." At the end of the day, all business growth and intellectual capital leveraging plans must revolve around a set of high-quality products and services that customers want and need.

CHAPTER 8

Harvesting the Power of Intellectual Capital Leveraging: Cooperatives, Customers, Channel Partners, Licensing, Joint Ventures, and Franchising

Innovations are created primarily by investment in intangibles. When such investments are commercially successful, and are protected by patents or first-mover advantages, they are transformed into tangible assets creating corporate value and growth.
—BARUCH LEV, PROFESSOR OF FINANCE, NEW YORK UNIVERSITY

For centuries, farmers have recognized the efficiencies of agricultural cooperatives. Cooperation and competition have been at odds with each other since the outset of the shift from the agricultural revolution to the industrial revolution. Entrepreneurs were rewarded for having products and services that their competitors did not offer. Scientists and engineers were rewarded with patents that granted exclusive rights to the use of their inventions. Researchers and professors who published widely were rewarded with tenure. But, as we shift from the industrial revolution to the digital revolution, we now live in a world where knowledge, best practices, wisdom, and data are more accessible than ever and the barriers to cooperation are slowly melting.

Companies have been forced to redefine business models, branding strategies, and cooperation policies in an era of social networking, open-source software development, and robust message boards and user groups. Scientists and engineers are moving away from "inward" problem solving to a more open or "broadcast" approach, and it is only a matter of time before business leaders and strategists follow. This trend toward working cohorts, cooperatives, consortiums, crowdsourcing, knowledge pooling, and cross-licensing will redefine intellectual property laws in a culture where people want to share with each other, both internally and externally, to drive the value of the institution as well as to foster improvements to the greater good—a heightened level of awareness or intelligence for our global society.

Cooperatives and Consortiums

At its core, a cooperative or consortium is a structure and a strategy that embraces the notion that many of us working together can achieve what one of us cannot individually. Why should each farmer growing oranges attempt to bring his output to the marketplace and establish channels and brand equity if it is easier, more cost-effective, and more efficient for them to band together, such as Sunkist? Some other industries have adapted cooperative business models as well, such as Ace hardware (centralized inventory ordering and consolidated advertising), Best Western hotels (centralized reservation system and consolidated branding), and EPIC pharmacies (centralized purchasing and marketing campaigns). Grapefruit and cranberry growers have done the same through Ocean Spray, as have almond farmers with Blue Diamond, grape growers with Welch's, and dairy farmers with Land 'O' Lakes. This has also occurred in the health-care, financial services, hospitality, funeral home, child-care, education, insurance, and housing industries. In some cases, research and development (R&D) resources have been pooled, often sharing resources and questions about missing puzzle pieces or creating research efficiencies or putting them in a better position to compete for grants. Other inventory-intense businesses, such as plumbing and lighting supplies, have formed cooperatives in order to negotiate better volume discounts, to increase their leverage with manufacturers, and to achieve distribution and inventory management efficiencies.

For a great resource on business cooperatives, visit the website of the National Cooperative Business Association (www.ncba.coop). The organization, founded in 1916, was known as the Cooperative League of America until 1922 and as the Cooperative League of the USA (CLUSA) until 1985. It was the first national organization for cooperatives. For nearly 80 years, NCBA has been dedicated to developing, advancing, and protecting cooperatives. It is the national voice for cooperatives, helping them compete in a changing economic and political environment.

In 2000, NCBA brought co-ops to the cutting edge of technology by successfully lobbying the Internet Corporation for Assigned Names and Numbers (ICANN) to create a new top-level Internet domain—.coop—exclusively for cooperatives. The .coop registry launched in January 2002 and now has more than 6,000 .coop Internet addresses representing dozens of industries using this innovative model.

Strategic cousins of the cooperative and consortium structure include federations, cohorts, buying groups, multiparty alliances, patent pooling, crowdsourcing, multilevel marketing plans, channel partnering, and, in some cases, even certain types of trade associations, clubs, and professional societies (depending on their historic roots).

Even as a society, we are moving toward an Internet-enabled pooling of collective knowledge and wisdom—from Wikipedia to P2P networks to message boards to comments posted on blogs and articles. All of these have facilitated "virtual" knowledge cooperatives and collaboration, as shown in Figure 8-1. This trend of commonly driven innovation is industrywide in areas such as software,

Figure 8-1. Our evolution toward a collective pooling of knowledge.

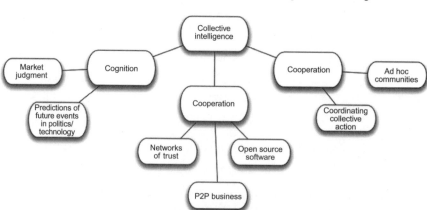

biotech, industrial design, environmental products, and agrichemicals and cross-disciplinary both horizontally and vertically. Scientists are more likely to "broadcast" a particular problem to a cross-disciplinary and diverse network, and their proposed solutions may come from a variety of resources. Innovation takes place both at the intersection of these disciplines and in deep industry verticals.

We seem to be sharing everything—from knowledge, in Wikipedia, Web 2.0, to cars and other forms of transport, with concepts like Zipcar and Velib, to DVDs, with concepts like Netflix (see Figure 8-2). Shared access to knowledge will drive more consortium and cooperative structures for harvesting intellectual capital in the future.

Patent Pooling

Today's intellectual capital agrarian must make the fundamental choice for each crop regarding the extent of the walls and fences

Figure 8-2. Types of harvesting strategies.

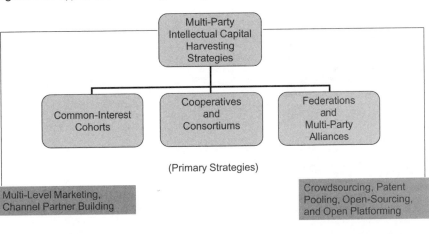

they will build to protect their properties, choosing from a wide array of strategic alternatives as articulated in Figure 8-2 and as explained in this chapter. Some companies around the globe have been rewarded for their vigilance in keeping properties, processes, systems, recipes, and best practices closely guarded by high concrete walls and impenetrable fences (e.g., KFC's 11 secret herbs and spices or the secret formula for Coca-Cola). Others use more transparent and porous picket fences and rancher's-gate-style walls and have adopted a more cooperative spirit, pooling their knowledge in the hope that shared knowledge will raise the value of all stakeholders in the group and that both markets and society can benefit from this community-driven approach.

These policies and legal strategies can be by invitation only, open ended and subject to a few rules or license/participation agreements, or completely open-turf. For example, while Apple clearly owns the technology driving the iPhone, hundreds of thousands of entrepreneurs and growing companies have been "invited" and encouraged to develop applications for the iPhone user under license and revenue-sharing agreements. This spirit of cooperation has been wildly successful for Apple (which has shifted the cost and creativity burden to thousands of fertile minds), for the developers of applications (which avoid the significant cost of building the hardware and the platform but earn revenues by developing the playthings and activities that sit atop the playground), and for the pride-gushing user community (which sits in line for up to 24 hours for the privilege of buying Apple's latest version of the iPhone).

This same mutually beneficial spirit has guided the recent proliferation of patent pooling, which is a form of a technology cooperative or consortium. In a patent pool, companies blend their patents with those of other companies. These pools allow users to access a number of companies' patents simultaneously, thereby avoiding the "patent thicket." In many cases, the pooling agreements also specify the pricing schedule in the agreement that establishes the pool, ensuring that no party can attempt to extract very high fees or to increase its fees after users are locked in. To survive antitrust scrutiny and for general strategies purposes, patent owners contributing to the pool typically reserve the right to license their patents outside the scope and focus of the pool.

Patent pools date back to as far as the 1850s (with the development of the 1856 sewing machine pool) but have proliferated in recent years, overcoming antitrust challenges and concerns along the way and driven by both the desire to efficiently conserve resources and the ability to more effectively communicate and collaborate over some networks. Proprietary products and services covered by patent pools were valued at $100 billion in the United States in 2000, while multiple standard-setting bodies today cover virtually every high-technology product. Moreover, the scope of these activities is likely to grow in future years. In many industries, leaders have expressed frustration about the proliferation of patent thickets—the large number of overlapping awards—and the ensuing rise of costly and time-consuming litigation. In many cases, technology sharing has been proposed as a remedy.

The scope of industries considering adopted patent pools has also grown. While patent pools have been well established in basic manufacturing and electronic industries for decades, they have also been seen as a potential solution for increasingly prevalent patent licensing issues elsewhere, such in new biotechnology-related fields. For instance, a great deal of interest has surrounded proposals to use patent pools to address the multiplicity of rights that is slowing research in diseases such as AIDS and breast cancer.

Patent pools are not only a way in which companies share their technology with each other. The rapid growth of open-source software during the first decade of the twenty-first century has been highlighted in numerous press accounts. The multibillion-dollar initial public offering of Red Hat and VA Linux, IBM's embrace of open-source and its investment of billions of dollars into these projects, and the recent (though qualified) embrace of Linux by Microsoft, formerly a bitter opponent, all have been extensively documented. What is much less well appreciated is that open-source is only the tip of the iceberg of the technology sharing that is reshaping high-technology industries. Patent pools, standard-setting organizations, and technology licensing efforts are having a profound effect on how companies seek to exploit new discoveries.

A variety of dynamic firms have catalyzed the establishment of patent pools, where firms with different agendas make their patents available on common terms. One example is MPEG-2, a digital video compression standard used in products including DVD and high-definition television. The standard was developed by the International Organization for Standardization, but during the completion of the standard-setting process, intellectual property issues became a paramount concern. The MPEG-2 patent pool was thus formed in 1993 to develop a unified approach to licensing. Led by CableLabs, an R&D consortium for the cable industry, the group established a patent pool that almost all the key players in the industry joined, despite the different incentives among pool members. This seems to have greatly facilitated the adoption of the MPEG-2 standard.

Open Sourcing and Open Platforming

In an agrarian approach that is more akin to Woodstock, some firms have taken a contrary approach to building bigger walls and stronger fences to protect their turf in favor of letting everyone and anyone onto their property to join the party. In this type of agrarian strategy, technology firms fully open their strategic kimonos and shift their business models and strategic focus to a more community-driven innovation platform.

A number of firms have taken the radical step of adopting a code release strategy, where companies release some existing proprietary code and then crate a governance structure for the resulting open-source development process. For example, IBM released half a million lines of its Cloudscape program, a simple database that resides inside a software application instead of as a full-fledged database program, to the Apache Software Foundation. And Hewlett-Packard released its Spectrum Object Model-Linker to the open-source community to help the Linux community write software to connect Linux with Hewlett-Packard's RISC computer architecture. This strategy is similar to giving away the razor (the release code) in order to sell more razor blades (the related consulting services that IBM and HP hope to provide).

If you decide to follow this approach toward community and user-based innovation, here are some guidelines and best practices for effective cooperative agrarianism:

* **Governance.** Be clear as to who decides what, where, and how. Determine how deadlocks will be broken.

* **Funding.** Be clear as to how and from whom funding will be raised to accomplish the goals and objectives of the cooperative. This is especially true after initial funding phases, such as when a "capital call" is necessary.

* **Staffing.** Ask questions about how the cooperative or community will be staffed. How will co-op members be selected? At whose expense? How will their performance be evaluated?

* **Lines of Demarcation.** Be sure the community understands what belongs to you alone and what is truly open-platform and shared by everyone.

* **Improvements.** Be clear as to the rules of engagement and participation. What are the rules for playing in the sandbox? Who owns improvements, new editions, and so on?

Crowdsourcing and the Wisdom of Crowds

When Regis Philbin, the host of *Who Wants to Be a Millionaire?*, encouraged the game show participants to "ask the audience" and a split second later a poll was produced to help contestants with their "final answer," a whole new form of intellectual capital agrarianism was born! Although it would be fun to actually credit Regis with pioneering this approach, effective intellectual capital agrarians have been "asking the audience" for feedback on product development, product design, distribution channels, customer service, branding, contests, and couponing for many years. Later in this chapter, we will look at the customer innovation centers being built by 3M, Pitney Bowes, and IBM around the world. But the growth of Web 2.0 has significantly increased the capability and proliferation of crowdsourcing, fan pages, and other trends.

The impact of social networking, Web 2.0, and crowdsourcing tools and strategies is now critical to overall branding, positioning, and awareness in areas from overall corporate strategy to basic couponing. Today, it is critical to have a presence on all major social networking sites such as Facebook, LinkedIn, Yelp,

Ning, and Flickr, including social networks abroad. Your goal is not only to accumulate "friends" but also to establish FanPages for a community that follows developments in your company. Mobile Internet marketing and advertising budgets, likely to reach $3.3 billion by 2013, were already a robust $648 million in 2008. The AppStore for the Apple iPhone offered more than 100,000 programs as of winter 2010, and these have been downloaded well over 1 billion times. The International Association for the Wireless Telecommunications Industry (known by its old acronym, the CTIA) estimates that more than 120 billion text messages are sent per month, well over 1 trillion per annum.

Consider these facts:

* Social networking sites overtook personal e-mail in June 2010 as the third most common use of the Internet. Business e-mail is at #2. You know what's still #1.

* The fastest-growing demographic is adults between the ages of 35 and 49, and the fastest growing applications are those for business purposes.

* People are just as inclined to "e-mail" you via a LinkedIn or Facebook account as they are to use a corporate system and to find you on company websites.

* As of May 2011, Facebook had nearly 600 million worldwide users in 40 languages (up from 50 million in January 2008—a more than 10-fold growth in just 34 months).

* As of November 2010, there were 175 million tweeters on Twitter, a 1,300 percent growth rate since January 2008.

* LinkedIn reached 100 million members in March 2011, adding nearly one million new users a week in 2011.

* If you want to "bookmark" (share) an article you read (or wrote) on the Internet, you have more than 50 sites or services to choose from (e.g., Digg, Reddit, Propeller, Technocrati, Faves, Kaboodle).

Social media and crowdsourcing-driven innovation strategies also include a presence on Wikipedia and other community-built information sites and a network on business-driven networking sites such as LinkedIn and Plaxo. In addition, social media and crowdsourcing can include posting content from your team as well as from satisfied customers on YouTube and other content-sharing websites. Social media innovation strategies include the preparation and dissemination of blogs (or podcasts or Web-casts) on a weekly or biweekly basis to stay in front of your target audiences as a thought leader and to keep them informed of new developments. Blogs help drive traffic to your website and can be optimized with keyword phrases for RSS (Really Simple Syndication) feeds, tagged for the technocratic audience, and uploaded instantly to your Facebook and MySpace sites. Interested readers can blog about your blog or include hyperlinks to your blog, website, or social networking pages. Online contests, promotions, coupons, and similar tools can be part of these postings as well to drive more traffic to your website to increase customer- or channel-partner-driven innovation and crowdsourcing.

Many companies have followed this basic concept for product innovation, real-time production, and customer feedback. One market leader is Zazzle, a New York City–based company that started out a few years ago offering t-shirts designed by the customer and made in real time, thereby reducing costs and inventory. Zazzle has since expanded its product lines to include a wide variety of custom products designed by the customer, from jackets to merchandise to offer products; it boasts more than 36.7 million choices on its website. Is this a trend? I plugged the phrase "custom products designed by you" into Google, and it pulled up more than 71 million hits!

Keene Addington, president of Flat Top Grill, a Chicago-based restaurant chain, is an example of an entrepreneur who uses social media to stay close to his customers and to seek ideas. In January 2011, he assigned a full-time marketing person to chat via e-mail and Twitter with as many of the chain's 75,000 customers as possible. One customer suggested serving make-your-own wraps prepared with lettuce. These wraps are now the chain's most popular appetizer.

For the Canadian shoemaker John Fluevog, customers do more than make suggestions—they design the products. Fluevog runs an "open-source footwear" project. Anyone can submit shoe designs to an online community of customers who vote on their favorites. In the past several years, Fluevog has received more than 1,000 design ideas and turned a dozen of them into market-able shoes. Fluevog took the open-source concept one step further by asking customers to vote on which of his existing lines should be cut or retained and on which print ads to run. Whatever the majority says, the company does. After customers voted on color combinations for the Sencha T-strap high heel, it became one of the best-selling shoes of the fall 2007 season. Despite the recession, the 115-employee company continues to grow its same-store and wholesale sales.

The old-fashioned employee or customer suggestion boxes that used to sit on the register counters of stores and in the lunchrooms at companies have been replaced and empowered by hypersteroids in a Web 2.0–driven environment. No longer are websites one-way communication tools that are really nothing more than online brochures. Today's sites are interactive and dynamic, providing tools, forums, postings, networks, user groups, and more vehicles for deeper and wider communication by and among the stakeholders (customers, vendors, suppliers, competitors, industry observers, media, academics) that all make up your company's ecosystem. Opportunities for break-through and incremental innovation at the business-model, product, or distribution level are no longer about periodic focus groups or annual user-group meetings or fishing through the suggestion box for the "ratchet-wrench big idea." Today's sources of innovation and feedback are more likely to come from a Facebook fan page, a LinkedIn user group, an industry-observing blogger, a posting on MySpace, a video on YouTube, a text message on BBM or ICQ, or a happy or unhappy "tweet" on Twitter. Today's consumer has the ability to communicate her opinion about her latest meal, the newest song or film, the most recent episode of her favorite television series, the experience she just had at a retail store, or her musings on an ex-boyfriend in hundreds of ways and on dozens of platforms, all of which must be carefully monitored by companies of all sizes and in all industries.

If you try to control or influence the message in this new democratized society, it may come back to haunt you. On the other hand, if you ignore it completely, you are likely to miss out on a variety of opportunities for learning and improvement and will be left way behind in the marketplace. If you find just the right balance between influence and listening, you could get yourself elected as the next U.S. president, as the Obama campaign found out after it executed an orchestrated Web 2.0 plan in 2008.

Building Effective Multiple-Channel Partner Relationships

Agrarians around the world know that production and distribu-tion must work hand in hand or there will be severe consequences and a halt to productivity. During the 2010 harvest, the *Hindustan* in Delhi reported that more than 67,000 tons of grain had rotted, just in the states of Punjab and Haryana, due to inefficient distribution channels. In a world where millions are dying of hunger and in a nation where more than 42 percent of the people live below the poverty line (World Bank Study, June 2005), how could such a gap in the infrastructure and efficiency of distribution channels exist? Innovation must be applied not only to the means of production but also to the means of distribution. Effective infrastructure, transparent channel partners, and incentives must be in place to bring needed goods and services to a hungry marketplace ready to consume.

Frustration over the rotting of much-needed grain is not limited to agricultural settings. Thousands of companies in hundreds of industries around the globe have inventories of "rotting" intellectual capital because of the same distribution inefficiencies and internal red tape. Markets hungry for solutions and new products and services are underserved because stale or broken or dysfunctional channels of distribution are in place that serve as a logjam and impede progress. What steps need to be taken within the broader industries and specific companies to unclog this drain? Who will take the lead and be accountable for distribution channel overhaul, training, support, incentive retailing, and transportation logistics to ensure that market demands are met and new revenue opportunities are uncovered? Who will ensure that our planet's intellectual capital is not rotting on the vine or in grain silos when it could be feeding hungry hearts and minds?

One step toward a solution is for every reader of this book to commit to a holistic and strategic undertaking of a channel and distribution partner effectiveness audit, which asks critical questions such as:

* How, when, and why was this channel built? Are the reasons for establishing the channel still relevant?

* Are the channel partners still invigorated and motivated to perform at optimum levels? Or have the relationships grown old, tired, and stale?

* Are the key economic premises underlying the channel still providing mutual rewards, incentives, and penalties for nonperformance? Or has the compensation model failed to evolve or serve its purpose?

* Are geographic allocations, protections, or preferences still relevant? Have they kept up with demographic shifts or current trends? Are territories too large or too small?

* What programs are in place to support, strengthen, and train the channel to perform at higher levels? Are today's training methodologies and technologies being used to share best practices and new product/service roll-outs? Or will it be another second-rate motivational speaker at this year's annual rubber chicken dinner at the annual meeting?

* Do the legal structure and the agreements between you and your channel partners still make sense? Are they agents or distributors? Are they authorized or certified in some fashion? Should a distribution system that lacks performance or loyalty be converted into a business-format franchise system? By you directly? By an authorized third party?

* Is the end consumer being properly served? Is the channel still competitive relative to its peers? How much loyalty or fidelity is expected from the channel, and what is its ability to carry products and services offered by your competitor?

The new agrarian must be committed to establishing, maintaining, and supporting the most innovative, efficient, and high-performing channels of distribution. Innovation in the board room or even on the factory floor will not ultimately drive shareholder value if it does not also manifest itself into efficient channels of trade and value-added ways to reach the targeted end consumer. If you build it, they won't come if they don't know you exist or don't know how to find you. And, without excellent customer service, they won't come back again. Innovation in branding, channel building, and customer service and support must all be a part of the new agrarian's playbook and almanac.

Today's intellectual agrarian faces a number of strategic and relationship management issues related to the development of channels, ranging from their initial establishment to the selection of appropriate channel partners to the growth of the channel as a whole and the individual growth of partnered organizations. There are also many challenges to be addressed regarding the development and maintenance of multiple channels and the various types of channel partners contained therein.

Channel partner relationships can make or break a company. If the agents that you rely upon to effectively reach the end customer—whether dealers, distributors, systems integrators, value-added resellers, agents, or franchisees in the value chain— are broken, stale, underperforming, unfocused, unappreciative, unimaginative, lazy, bored, or unfaithful, that will have a direct and harmful impact on your brand, your shareholder value, and your bottom line. If time, attention, and resources are focused on nurturing and supporting these relationships, then the company is very likely to meet and exceed its growth objectives. The role and importance of a strong channel partner program as a critical growth priority cannot be underestimated.

Companies of all sizes and in all industries face many challenges when attempting to build a healthy and profitable set of channel relationships. Channel builders and channel killers are highlighted in Figure 8-3. These include:

* Fostering channel loyalty and performance in a fast-moving and highly competitive domestic and global marketplace

Figure 8-3. Variables that strengthen/weaken distribution channels.

Channel Builders	Channel Killers
• Communicates on a regular and meaningful basis • Selects partners for their ability to bring new capabilities and to open up new markets (e.g., federal government sales) on behalf of the mothership • Supports R&D/innovation leading to real desired and desired new product lines and enhancements • Supports value-added field support and education • Seeks innovative solutions primarily from the channel partners and not just from the mothership • Performs regular channel partner effectiveness audits and market-by-market analysis • Constantly focuses on the *real* needs of the end customers and competitive forces	• Presence of politics and turf wars • Allows partners to become "fat and lazy" • Fails to eliminate the deadwood from the channel • Existence of designated territories that are too big or too small • Talks to each other only when there is a problem (instead of proactively and regularly brainstorming opportunities) • Fails to understand, recognize, and support "micromarket" differences in channel partner territories • Allows annual golf and steak dinner conferences as a substitute for service value-added support

* Maintaining and growing mindshare and increasing loyalty among your channel partners as a competitive advantage

* Eliminating flat channel performance in terms of sales, new product roll-out and adoption, or market penetration caused by lack of support, burnout, or complacency

* Decreasing the cost of maintaining a partnership while increasing channel effectiveness

* Focusing too much on top-down growth objectives from the channel creator, rather than on building and strengthening channel partner relationships and profitability from the bottom up

* Failing to achieve alignment on and to communicate goals, objectives, and performance metrics by and between corporate headquarters and the individual channel partner

* Overemphasizing sales training and new product roll-outs with little or no commitment to basic business management, ongoing growth training, and overall channel health

* Failing to allocate corporate channel resources in an effective manner to boost support, training, and financial performance within partner organizations

* Analyzing current channel performance and divesting unproductive channel relationships to focus channel management's time, effort, and financial resources on building profitable relationships and encouraging new, high-potential partnerships

When building an effective set of channel relationships, the following strategic questions must be considered:

* How much time, energy, and monetary resources have you invested in analyzing the success of your current channel relationships?

* What is the functionality of current channels?

* How do you currently bring your products and services to the marketplace?

* Are you getting the most out of your current channel partners?

* How do you determine a successful channel relationship, and how do you approach an underperforming relationship?

* What steps are you taking to manage, motivate, educate, and communicate with your channel partners?

* How does your approach differ in your interactions with established and new or future partners?

* What steps have you taken recently to strengthen and support the channel?

* Have you developed a systematic approach to collaboration on both a horizontal and a vertical level?

* Have you reached clarity and agreement with each of your channel partners as to each party's objectives, strategy, commitment, and capabilities?

* Are clear goals and performance metrics in place with each of your partners?

* How often are these goals and metrics reviewed and reevaluated?

* How have global business norms and cultural differences impacted the effectiveness of your channel partner relationships?

* Have you recently evaluated channel performance on a partner-by-partner basis? Are minimum standards in place? Why or why not? Are minimum standards enforced? What are the consequences if they are not met?

* What competitive choices do your channel partners have as alternatives to your products or services, and how are you identifying, maintaining, and improving your competitive advantage?

* Is the business model underlying the channel partner relationship working well? Neutral? Broken?

* Are there horizontal or vertical conflicts within the channel? If yes, what types of conflicts have been arising? How? When? At what cost?

* How insulated are you from the end customer? Has this communication barrier hurt product development?

Many intellectual capital agrarians offer sales team training to channel partners, but very few channel builders or managers devote the needed resources to support and train channel partners to ensure that their businesses are growing properly. This training aims to provide significant added value through existing relationships between the company and its channel partners and should be designed in accordance with the guidelines in Figure 8-4. As we well know, stronger relationships and stronger channel partners can lead to significant enhancement of the bottom line.

Figure 8-4. Improving channel partner performance through dynamic and targeted training.

At the core, channel partner training programs should be focused on: (1) the *support* of your strongest partners ("A players"); (2) the *improvement* of your average partners ("B players"); and (3) the *turnaround* of your weakest channel partners ("C players"). Intellectual capital agrarians must develop channel partner training programs to address the needs of each type of channel partner in your system, as well as a transition strategy for C players who are unable to be rehabilitated. A simple transformation of a reasonable number of C players into B players and B players into A players can significantly enhance channel performance and overall company profitability.

Characteristics of Partner	Focus of Training	Goals
Strongest of the A players	Strategic planning Expansion strategies	Keep them strong, loyal, motivated, and focused Gather and analyze "best practices"
A players who have lost focus or who suffer from relationship staleness, laziness, or boredom	Succession planning Business planning Realignment of goals	Reinvigorate their commitment Bring new initiatives and fresh ideas to the table
B players with A player potential	Business planning and capital formation Building effective teams Coaching and mentoring to get to the next level	Provide them with the tools for growth Mentor them into A players
Underperforming B players	Motivation and analysis of underperformance	Analyze growth hurdles and challenges Set goals and perform organizational analysis
Underperforming B players	Business planning fundamentals Strategic performance audit Leadership and management coaching	Perform deep analysis to get them to B level Focus intently on business plans and sales training
Weakest of the C players	Transition and phase-out	Terminate the relationship

Joint Ventures and Strategic Partnering

For more than 1,000 years, farmers of all kinds have relied on others to help them plant, irrigate, harvest, and bring their crops to the marketplace. It would be naive, arrogant, and inefficient to assume that any one farmer could succeed without establishing strategic and mutually beneficial relationships with a wide variety of others who share common goals and who are rewarded by successes and vice versa. Pioneers learned in the 1800s and 1900s to hitch their wagons to each other in order to share the burden and costs of exploring new territories and to better defend themselves against hostile attacks. And, while farmers have known this for centuries, corporations and industries have seemed to be waking up to this fact only over the past few decades.

During the industrial revolution, joint venture structures were often used in the railroad industry in the late 1800s. Throughout the middle part of the twentieth century, they were very common in the manufacturing sector. By the late 1980s, joint ventures increasingly appeared in the technology, medical, and service industries as businesses looked for new, competitive strategies. Between 1990 and 2000, there were 60,446 joint venture transactions around the globe, of which 60 percent had cross-border participants and 40 percent had domestic participants only.

As an intellectual capital leveraging strategy, joint ventures and alliances are dynamic partnerships that can be structured at the horizontal or the vertical level. They can be R&D driven, distribution driven, marketing and sales driven, human capital driven, or financially driven. They can be two-party or multiparty (though if many parties are involved, the venture is probably a cooperative or consortium, as discussed earlier in this chapter). They can be with direct competitors (subject to applicable antitrust laws), global parallel industry peers, and even those outside your industry or with various parties in your supply or distribution chain. They can be open ended or close ended. They can also be driven by a need to thrive or by a need to survive, as in the case of "distressed" joint ventures, such as that of Chrysler and Fiat during the recession of 2009. They also can be known as strategic partnering, cross-licensing, co-branding, or technology transfer agreements. The objective is typically to accomplish one or more of the following: (1) to get a direct capital infusion in exchange for equity and/or intellectual property or distribution rights; (2) to create a "capital substitute" where the resources that would otherwise be obtained with the capital are obtained through joint venturing; or (3) to shift the burden and cost of development (through licensing) in exchange for a potentially more limited upside.

These various types of partnering arrangements have been used for a wide variety of business purposes and to meet intellectual capital leveraging objectives, including joint research and co-promotion; distribution and commercialization (particularly between defense and government contractors looking for new applications and markets for products initially developed for the military and governmental sectors); and cross-licensing and sublicensing of new technologies. The participants to these agreements can be at various points in the value chain or distribution channel, and deals can range from agreements by and among direct or potential competitors (e.g., to cooperate rather than compete as a precursor to a merger and/or to join forces to fend off an even larger competitor) to agreements by and among parallel producers (e.g., to widen or integrate product lines) to linking parties at different points in the vertical distribution channel (e.g., to achieve distribution efficiencies).

Innovation and Partnering at the Customer Level

An open-ended vertical strategic partnering approach that was pioneered by 3M in 1997 is now a model for customer-centric partnering-driven innovation around the world. While the company achieved its most prominent consumer brand recognition with its canary-colored Post-it notes, it has been operating and innovating in a wide variety of industry segments and producing or co-producing profitable products for decades, in the transportation, electronics, health-care, safety and security, and home and leisure industries. In 2009, 3M opened its first open-ended customer innovation center in Sumitomo, Japan, to foster innovation by getting and staying close to its customers—both strategically and literally. Reversing the Web 2.0 and social networking trend toward online customer interaction, the company relies on physical building and good old-fashioned face-to-face interactions to help stimulate new ideas and product development. It is striving to have a deep understanding of customer needs, consuming patterns, and preferences as primary sources of innovation, which is a lesson and a strategy that we can all learn from.

3M now operates 23 customer innovation centers around the world, from Brazil to India to Russia to China to Dubai. These centers are often located near 3M's own research facilities in order to ensure collaboration, communication, and data sharing without silos or politics. As 3M has discovered, there is a big difference between employing hands-on interactions with customers to learn what they are truly trying to accomplish and taking an online survey that awkwardly asks customers what they allegedly need. This commitment has not only given rise to new product ideas and improvements but also led to joint ventures and alliances with a wide variety of customers, including a partnership with Vistean to develop lighting and film technologies to redefine the look and functionality of automobile dashboards.

Other companies in different industries have followed 3M's lead. Hershey opened its first customer innovation center in 2006 with a focus on retail customers. The center includes a tasting facility and a mock store where merchandising ideas are tested and refined. The overall shopping experience is monitored and studied under a microscope. Pitney Bowes opened its first customer innovation center in 2009 in Shelton, Connecticut, where the centerpiece of activity was the company's new IntelliJet color pointing system. In the Pitney Bowes Center, customers are invited to interact with the new system and share their hands-on observations and are able to load their own custom applications onto the system, which has had a direct impact on future new product development, as well as incremental improvements in existing products. Many other global technology companies have followed suit. IBM has its Business Partner Innovation Center, which showcases IBM System Group and Software Group solutions to customers who have the opportunity to learn, assess, design, and test the entire family of IBM's hardware and software products and solutions. The hands-on testing by customers provides IBM with the confidence it needs regarding its solutions prior to their "live" implementation.

In March 2005, Xerox opened its Gil Hatch Center for Customer Innovation, which is designed to give current and prospective customers one-stop access to its entire portfolio of digital production printing equipment and solutions. The facility, which employs more than 60 people and hosts several thousand customers a year, provides customers with a place to test applications, receive training, and showcase their own innovations. Wrigley opened its global innovation center in Chicago, Illinois, in May 2005. Its focus on creativity and collaboration allows the acceleration of promoting and marketing throughout the world. By bringing consumer-driven innovation into its company, Wrigley was able to rapidly advance as a mainstream confectionery company and was purchased by Mars in 2009, a company long committed to staying close to its end consumers with multiple innovations around its M&M brands.

Joint Ventures and Strategic Alliances: Davids and Goliaths

Around the globe, there are multiple opportunities for strategic partnering between larger companies (the "Goliaths") and smaller ones (the "Davids") that can help both parties be more effective intellectual capital agrarians and drive shareholder value. It is often the case that a larger partner brings the capital, human resources, and channels and that the smaller company needs to bring its new products and services to the marketplace, creating an interdependent relationship where decisions regarding governance, budgeting, staffing, ownership, dispute resolution, and many other issues must be made before the relationship is formally consummated. For the Davids, it is critical to establish an internal champion that can be a strategic point of contact for the company as it competes for attention with the thousands of other projects that may be going on inside the Goliaths. It is also critical to establish mutual respect, rapport, and trust, especially with respect to the handling and ownership of David's intellectual capital. For the Goliaths, it is critical to have an exit plan should there be a shift in strategic direction or a change in leadership that renders the joint venture or alliance no longer relevant or of strategic importance, as well as an upside plan, often an acquisition, should the project wildly exceed everyone's expectations or should the products that are jointly developed prove to offer a significant competitive advantage.

For many leaders of early-stage and emerging growth companies (e.g., the Davids), joint ventures and alliances are not the only ways to engage or dance with a Goliath. In fact, Goliath may have a formal or informal investment fund for direct strategic and venture capital–"style" investments in smaller companies. Another interesting aspect of intellectual capital agrarianism for Davids is to determine which technologies or initiatives within Goliaths have been recently abandoned and essentially adopt them via licensing, purchase spin-offs, or partnering. These technologies are often referred to as "widows and orphans" in that, often, millions of dollars in time and effort have been invested in a given technology or project, but, for reasons ranging from shifts in leadership or strategic direction to lack of budgeting to internal politics to a loss of an engineering team to a competitor or a cutback, the Goliath has temporarily or permanently abandoned the project. In other cases, the Goliath may have acquired multiple portfolios of intellectual capital via acquisition but have been interested in a particular portfolio, leaving it with valuable crops that are rotting on the vine with no caretakers or budget allocation. It is typically the case that Davids can get access or even ownership of these assets at a significantly reduced price or royalty rate, since they are merely collecting dust in their current state. And, as we have established, Goliaths owe fiduciary obligations to their shareholders to find harvestable revenue streams from these intangible properties.

Some Davids are very passive and reactive when it comes to establishing relationships with Goliaths and others are much more proactive. For those that are passive and reactive, it can be a long and arduous process to find the right person to contact to discuss the possibility of a strategic relationship. In some cases, there is a specific person or department in charge of evaluating proposals from smaller companies, and such a person or department is usually but not always the best place to start.

At other Goliaths, the contact may be more situational or anecdotal; a conversation between a company rep and an ordinary supplier, vendor, customer, or distributor evolves into a relationship that is more meaningful and strategic. In other areas, such as government contracting or biotechnology, teaming and strategic partnerships are a very common way of harvesting intellectual capital or processing new contractual opportunities, especially if they are mandated by federal procurement regulations. And it is not just federal guidelines that are driving teaming, subcontracting, and mentor-protégé relationships among the Davids and Goliaths. In some cases, the research and development budgets and teams inside technology and defense Goliaths have led them to depend on small companies for new ideas and technologies. Whether internally or by default, these Goliaths have essentially "outsourced" new-product development and innovation to their smaller counterparts. From the Davids' perspective, the access to resources and the speed to the market that a partnership with a Goliath can offer are difficult to ignore. Goliaths' unwillingness to commit resources to innovation or foster a culture of creativity has created a dependence on smaller partners to fill this gap and keep them competitive. For emerging growth companies, the chance to be the "skunkworks" operations for companies unwilling or unable to do the research for themselves can be a significant opportunity, allowing the eccentric and free-spirited inventor or entrepreneur to remain independent and not be absorbed into a culture where he would likely not survive for more than a week.

In a recent and encouraging trend, larger companies have actively been seeking strategic relationships with smaller companies in a proactive fashion. Look at the relationship that Apple has cultivated with thousands of smaller and more entrepreneurial developers of applications for its iPhone and iPad products. And, in late 2010, Wal-Mart announced an aggressive partnering and purchasing program to foster greater distribution opportunities for local and sustainable food farmers. Wal-Mart's new initiative is designed to open up more supply relationships with smaller food producers and includes investment in training and infrastructure for small and medium-size farmers, particularly in emerging markets. Wal-Mart hopes to buy at least 30 percent of its produce from small local farmers by 2013.

There was a great IBM advertisement years ago that reminds us that David and Goliaths need each other and often underestimate the value that they can bring to one another. The scenes went something like the diagram in Figure 8-5.

Figure 8-5. The irony of innovation ideation.

Big Co Conglomerate

Mid-sized Company

Rapid Growth Small Company

Two Guys in a Garage

Problem Arises

I wonder what the two guys in a garage would do?

I wonder what the guys at Big Co Conglomerate would do?

I wonder what the guys at a Mid-sized Company would do?

I wonder what the leaders of the Rapid Growth Company would do?

Best Practices in Joint-Ventures Formation and Management: Dow Chemical

For companies truly committed to being intellectual capital agrarians, the process of establishing joint ventures and strategic alliances comes naturally—the assumption is that they alone do not have all of the solutions, the channels, the know-how, and the human resources to fully maximize shareholder value, so the idea that it makes sense to partner with others to drive synergies and supply missing puzzle pieces is embedded in their corporate strategy and culture. Best practices in establishing joint ventures require a shared vision, a jointly developed business plan, and a discipline in the establishment and management of these complex relationships.

Let's take a look at an excerpt of a Dow Chemical White Paper on Joint Ventures that was published in April 2008:

Joint ventures, or nonconsolidated affiliates, play an integral role in Dow's strategy to dampen earnings cyclicality and improve earnings growth. In recent years, the financial contribution of our joint ventures has grown significantly. In 2007, equity earnings rose to $1.1 billion, exceeding $1 billion for the first time in the Company's history, while cash distributions from joint ventures topped $800 million, setting another record for the Company. This White Paper is intended to provide greater clarity around Dow's joint venture activities and their value proposition to Dow, with a specific focus on the Company's principal nonconsolidated affiliates, or principal joint ventures, numbering around a dozen in total. In 2007, these principal joint ventures accounted for over 90 percent of Dow's total equity earnings and cash distributions from nonconsolidated affiliates.

As Dow pursues a strategy focused on improving earnings growth and consistency, joint ventures are a crucial enabler, creating opportunities to accelerate the Company's strategic agenda across several different dimensions. Dow has established a number of joint ventures with upstream partners focused specifically on developing highly competitive, world scale production facilities with access to cost-advantaged feedstocks. Dow brings technology, operational know-how, global reach and product diversity. Its partners bring cost-advantaged feedstocks, upstream expertise, local market presence and/or regional perspective. This combination delivers a significant competitive edge to each joint venture.

One of Dow's uses of joint ventures is directly tied to harvesting existing intellectual assets. Take a look at this excerpt from the White Paper:

The Company has strengthened the market position and future growth potential of several of its commodity businesses by placing existing Dow assets into newly formed joint ventures. For Dow, this carve-out model retains the value of integration, while reducing capital investment and further shifting the Company's portfolio balance towards the Performance businesses. Additional value is also derived by working with partners that bring specific strengths, such as back integration to feedstocks or an expanded geographic presence. And in some cases, the formation of a joint venture also generates substantial cash for Dow, with which the Company can pursue investment opportunities focused on its performance businesses. The Company's joint venture model has helped Dow to build its presence in several important geographic regions, providing access to areas that were either restricted by regula-

(continues)

tion or constrained by well-established supplier relationships. Partnering with local companies, the Company has been able to swiftly develop brand and market presence, while creating in-country manufacturing capability for a joint venture, which can derive significant value from Dow's technology and operational expertise.

Dow has also used joint ventures to foster new technology development, as the following excerpt indicates:

Joint ventures can provide a vital platform for technology development, defining a structure that enables full collaboration between Dow and its selected partners, as well as creating a mechanism for effective commercialization. The Company has formed several joint ventures through the years with organizations both inside and outside the chemical industry, specifically focused on delivering technology breakthroughs that neither party could achieve alone. Dow has gained a tremendous amount of respect within the world of global chemical companies for its know-how, technology, operational excellence, global reach, cultural understanding, product breadth, and market positions/channels. This makes Dow an attractive partner to companies around the globe that wish to get into the chemicals arena, allowing the Company to select from a range of attractive opportunities. Dow's joint venture portfolio has tremendous global reach. In 2007, nearly 75 percent of Dow's proportionate share of joint venture sales went to customers outside North America—with 39 percent in Asia Pacific. Joint ventures also contribute across the breadth of Dow's operating segments, with 40 percent of Dow's equity earnings coming from joint ventures as follows:

Basic Chemicals	36%
Performance Chemicals	34%
Basic Plastics	16%
Hydrocarbons & Energy	8%
Performance Plastics	6%
Agricultural Sciences	<1%

Drafting a Memorandum of Understanding Prior to Structuring the Joint Venture or Alliance Agreement

Prior to drafting the definitive joint venture or alliance agreement, it is very beneficial to hammer out a *Memorandum of Under-*

standing to reflect a business handshake on all critical points of the relationship and for the lawyers to use a starting point in the preparation of the formal agreements. (For more information on structuring these relationships, see Chapter 20 of my book *Franchising and Licensing: Two Powerful Ways to Grow Your Business in Any Economy*, 4th edition [AMACOM, 2011].) Here is an excerpted checklist from that book that can guide you through a discussion of the key elements:

* **Spirit and Purpose of the Agreement.** Outline why the partnering arrangement is being considered and what is its perceived mission and objectives. Describe "operating principles" that will foster communication and trust. What are the strategic and financial desires of the participants?

* **Scope of Activity.** Address what products, services, buildings, or other specific projects will be included and excluded from the venture. Identify target markets (i.e., regions, user groups, etc.) for the venture and any markets excluded from the venture that will remain the domain of the partners. If the venture has purchase and supply provisions, state that the newly-formed entity or arrangement will purchase or supply specific products, services, or resources from or to the owners.

* **Key Objectives and Responsibilities.** Clarify and specify objectives and targets to be achieved by the relationship, when to expect achieving these objectives, any major obstacles anticipated, and the point at which the alliance will be self-supporting, be brought out, or be terminated. Participants should designate a project manager who will be responsible for their company's day-to-day involvement in the alliance. If a separate detached organization will be created, the key persons assigned to the ven-

ture should be designated if practical. Responsibilities should be outlined to make it clear to other partners who will be doing what.

* **Method for Decision Making.** Each partnering relationship will have its own unique decision-making process. Describe who is expected to have the authority to make what types of decisions in what circumstances, who reports to whom, etc. If one company will have operating control, they should be designated at this point.

* **Resource Commitments.** Most partnering relationships involve the commitment of specific financial resources, such as cash, equity, staged payments, and loan guarantees, to achievement of the ultimate goals. Other "soft" resources may be in the form of licenses, knowledge, R&D, a sales force, contracts, production, facilities, inventory, raw materials, engineering drawings, management staff, access to capital, the devotion of specific personnel for a certain percentage of their time, etc. If possible, these "soft" resources should be quantified with a financial figure so that a monetary value can be affixed and valued along with the cash commitments to this internal commitment. In some circumstances, the purchase of buildings, materials, consultants, advertising, etc., will require capital. These external costs should be itemized and allocated between the partners in whatever formula is agreed. If any borrowing, entry into equity markets (public offerings, private placements, etc.), or purchase of stock in one of the partners is anticipated, these should be noted. In anticipation of additional equity infusions, the partners should agree about their own ability to fund the overruns or enable the venture to seek other outside sources. The manner of handling cost overruns should be addressed. Pricing and costing procedures should be mentioned if applicable.

* **Assumption of Risks and Division of Rewards.** What are the perceived risks? How will they be handled and who will be responsible for problem-solving and risk assumption? What are the expected rewards (e.g., new product, new market, cash flow, technology)? How will the profits be divided?

* **Rights and Exclusions.** Who has rights to products and inventions? Who has rights to distribute the products, services, technologies, etc.? Who gets the licensing rights? If the Confidentiality and Noncompetition Agreement have not yet been drafted in final form at this point, they should be addressed in basic form here. Otherwise, if the other agreements have been signed, simply make reference to these other agreements.

* **Anticipated Structure.** This section of the Memorandum of Understanding should describe the intended structure (written contract, corporation, partnership, or equity investment). Regardless of the legal form, the terms, percentages, and formulas for exchange of stock, if possible at this stage, should be spelled out. Default provisions and procedures should at least be addressed at the preliminary level.

Strategic Partnering and "the Last Mile"

In the cable television telecom industry, there is a strategic concept known as "the last mile." At the heart of this concept is the notion that you can lay thousands of miles of cable, but if you can't connect with the customers and communities as the ultimate source of revenue, then all of your time and efforts will have been wasted. It is one of the ultimate examples of the adage "don't confuse activity with results." When it comes to intellectual capital harvesting, what is the equivalent of the "last mile" in your business or industry? In other words, notwithstanding all of your impressive R&D or product development efforts, what will it really take to reach the end customer at her doorstep? Take a hard look at your current distribution channels and strategic partners. Are they truly your strong bond and connection to the end customer, adding value at every step? Or are these channels and relationships old, tired, stale, and burnt out? Are they capable of a restart, a reboot, or a retaking of the marriage vows? Or is it time to fully or partially overhaul channels and relationships to make sure that profitable revenue streams can be established and maintained?

Breaking Up Is Hard to Do

Collaboration with external partners is a critical component of intellectual capital agrarianism, but it is far from a panacea. Just as more than 50 percent of all marriages in the United States end in divorce, so, too, do corporate courtships. And the windup can be just as bitter, with fights over custody of the "children" and the allocation of the distribution of "marital" assets.

There is room for improvement in the way that all types of joint ventures and alliances are formed, structured, and dissolved. According to a 2008 Microsoft/PTRM study on innovation best practices, only 35 percent of the companies surveyed had a defined process in place for identifying the variables to consider when assessing whether to enter into a joint venture or alliance (often resulting in lost opportunities), and only a slightly better 44% had a process in place for identifying and selecting potential partners. A disturbing 60 percent had not clearly defined an exit strategy or a set of clear metrics or performance standards to use when determining whether a joint venture or alliance had been a success or failure. The lack of a "corporate prenuptial" or exit strategy complicates further what is already a messy situation and dilutes shareholder value creation for all involved parties. We can and must do better at strategic corporate matchmaking at all levels.

Licensing Strategies to Drive Revenues and Profits

The crops of an intellectual capital agrarian harvest have many applications in the marketplace. As we examined earlier in this chapter, they can serve as growth drivers at the heart of joint ventures, strategic alliances, and co-branding relationships. Another type of intellectual capital harvesting strategy is licensing. New revenues and opportunities can be generated by granting a license to use, make, sell or resell, or service/maintain a product; to operate a prescribed business format; to install or download software; or to advise, consult with, train, or support company staff (see Figure 8-6).

The "crops" of an intellectual capital harvest confer a wide range of legal rights that go with ownership, and, short of an absolute sale or transfer of all of them, your company may segregate, bucketize, and/or strategically use them as a source of new revenues, new opportunities, or new strategies to penetrate markets, new relationships, and new profit centers. And, as we will learn, you do not necessarily need to be the original farmer of these assets to create new opportunities. Intellectual capital agrarians also look for situations to jointly develop and harvest intellectual capital, to serve the licensee of the intellectual capital of others, or even to be the intermediary that harvests IP for third parties. Licensing is a contractual method of developing

Figure 8-6. Licensing strategies as a form of intellectual capital agrarianism.

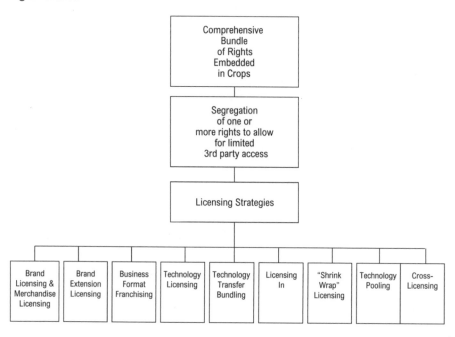

and exploiting intellectual property by transferring rights of use to third parties without the transfer of ownership. From a strategic perspective, it is the process of maximizing shareholder value by creating new income streams and market opportunities by uncovering the hidden or underutilized value in your portfolio of intellectual assets and finding licensees that will pay you for the privilege of having access and usage of this intellectual capital.

Overall Licensing Best Practices

As an intellectual capital leveraging strategy, the many types of licensing articulated in Figure 8-6 enjoy mixed success and inconsistent prioritization in large, medium-size, and small companies.

It can be actively exploited, benignly neglected, or anything in between. Research and development efforts may yield new product and service opportunities that are not critical to the company's core business lines or technologies that become technologic or strategic "widows" and "orphans" (e.g., lack internal support or resources) because of political reasons or changes in leadership or because the company simply lacks the expertise on the resources to bring the products or services to the marketplace. In other cases, the underlying technology may have multiple applications and usages, but the company does not have the time or resources to develop the technology beyond its core business. The better managed intellectual capital–driven companies will recognize these assets as still having significant value and develop licensing programs. Intellectual property licensing has become a powerful economic force. Since the federal circuit court system in 1982 established national uniformity and enforcement of patent laws, companies have come to recognize the value of patent licensing, and revenues are likely to quintuple in the United States between 1998 and 2015 to an estimated $500 billion. Royalty revenues from patent licensing were $15 billion in 1990 and skyrocketed to more than $350 billion in 2009.

Every year, intellectual capital agrarians such as IBM, GE, DuPont, and Texas Instruments generate billions of dollars in high-margin revenue streams, which not only offset their research and development costs but also help drive the quality of their earnings. These companies realize that not all applications or fruits of their technology harvest will be in core areas of focus for their internal divisions but that external third parties may benefit from access to their technology, systems, and innovations.

Licensing may be to direct competitors, to indirect competitors, to parties completely outside your industry, or to companies operating outside your currently signed markets, either domestic or international. You may also want to consider licensing to after-market providers that may need access to your technology or the use of your brands in areas such as training, support, repair, or maintenance. Business leaders should work with in-house and external legal and strategic advisers to develop licensing strategies and policies that will articulate key objectives, such as criteria for screening and selecting target licensees, prohibited practices, quality control and brand protection, degrees of exclusivity, royalty rates, metrics for success, performance standards, other sources of income, audits and inspections, and grounds for termination. The scope of the technology that will be made available for licensing should be clearly explained and technology that will be kept completely proprietary should be clearly excluded. Licensing policies and strategies should be aligned with overall corporate plans and goals of the company and communicated across divisional lines. Each licensing arrangement should be carefully managed and monitored to protect both quality control and to ensure timely royalty and other payments.

Due diligence regarding the capability of the licensee to execute its business plan; its track record, reputation, and integrity; its channels and markets; and its financial strength should be thoroughly conducted before formal arrangements are put in place. Granting rights to an unqualified or unreliable licensee will virtually ensure disputes down the road and may be expensive from an opportunity cost perspective if exclusive rights are granted in a given industry or target market. (For more information on developing a licensing strategy or structuring a licensing agreement, see Chapter 19 of my book *Franchising and Licensing: Two Powerful Ways to Grow Your Business in Any Economy*, 4th edition [AMACOM, 2011].)

Licensing In: Reaping What Others Sow

Not all licensing strategies involve leveraging your intellectual capital to others in exchange for royalties. In some cases, the growth can be driven by the licensing of stale, ignored, or under-developed technology or brands ("the widows and orphans") of another company. *Licensing in* (that is, acquiring the use of another company's product by entering into a contractual agreement that allows you to use that product in certain defined ways) can be used to add value or to fill in missing strategic puzzle pieces, enhance consumer recognition and loyalty, or serve as a strategic precursor to a joint venture or acquisition transaction.

In our Internet-driven digital age, it is easier than ever to uncover technologies that may be available for licensing by checking the websites of larger companies, EDGAR (the SEC's database on public companies) filings, research institutions and government agency postings, and other resources listed in the Appendix at the end of this book. For example, of the $51.47 billion spent in 2008 on R&D, our nation's universities collected in the aggregate only $3.4 billion, so it is clear that there are still tens of thousands of technologies still at the dance waiting for a partner. Some universities, agencies, and research labs are very proactive in their search for licensees and partners, but many are reactive and even resistant to the process. You will need to be the one to initiate contact and be persistent and proactive to help harvest their technology. Notwithstanding the excellent efforts of the Association of University Technology Managers (AUTM), Licensing Executives Society (LES) members, and groups like the Association of Small Business Development Centers (ASBDC), National Business Incubation Association (NBIA), and National Collegiate Inventors and Innovators Alliance (NCIIA) , there is still an incredible amount of university research that goes unharvested and noncommercialized each year. We must develop better systems and processes, a stronger entrepreneurial culture, a proactive attitude, more robust rewards, and more sharing of best practices in the fostering of partnerships between universities and the corporate world.

Licensing can be driven by brands or technology—it can take advantage of intellectual capital owned by others that can help complete your own strategic farming puzzle or serve as the catalyst or fertilizer for enhanced innovation within your company. The process need not be random; websites and databases now regularly deploy brands available for licensing, and some of these are listed in the Appendix.

And, speaking of orphans, it is not just technology that can be abandoned with no one to care for it. In December 2010, Brands USA Holdings held an auction of nearly 150 recognized trademarks, whose brands were attached to products and services that no longer exist but that could be revived by the successful bidders. Assets open to bidders included once-venerable brands such as Meister Brau (beer), Handi-Wrap (consumer goods), Braniff (airlines), Pom Poms (candy), Long & Silky/ Short & Sassy (hair care products), Lucky Whip (food toppings), Bowery (bank), Fruit Bombs (candy), and Snow Crop (frozen foods). We will have to wait and see what entrepreneurial strategies are deployed by the successful bidders as those assets are replanted, nurtured, and reharvested.

While there are additional database providers that serve the technology environment, the management of knowledge and the innovative process, the transfer of technology, and the inherent requirement for ultimate management of intellectual assets are functionally separate, and no single organization currently provides truly efficient comprehensive support to the market. Innovation is inherent in technology transfer, and effective management of the culture of innovation is fundamental to developing, integrating, or selling technology that will increase shareholder value. It is essential to the effective management or innovation that the products of such efforts be "codified" to the extent that they can be optimally focused on the mission of the sponsoring organization and in the context of both the internal and the external environments. The codification process is often met today with information systems solutions that capture information, organize it around related knowledge, warehouse it, and then enable the extraction of relevant portions for collaboration and research.

The concept of codifying knowledge assets in order to enable the efficient and effective creation, location, capture, and sharing of the knowledge and expertise that reside in an organization has been studied at length by a variety of knowledge management researchers. To that extent, the ability to collaborate, to access both internal and external resources, and to group or cluster codified knowledge information becomes an essential aspect of truly effective knowledge management. Innovation, collaboration, and codification are optimized in the context of a knowledge strategy that examines value opportunities, business cases, and the internal structures for development, all of which can serve at the heart of a multifaceted licensing strategy and at the core of a commitment to intellectual capital agrarianism.

Franchising

Over the past few decades, franchising has emerged as a leading intellectual capital harvesting strategy for a variety of product and service companies operating in more than 100 diverse industries at various stages of development. Recent International Franchise Association ("IFA") Educational Foundation statistics demonstrate that retail sales from franchised outlets account for more than 50 percent of all retail sales in the United States, with total economic output (including gross sales) estimated at more than $2.3 trillion. Franchises employed more than 21 million people at more than 900,000 establishments in 2009. In an era when unemployment was running around 9 percent and underemployment was at nearly 20 percent, franchised businesses provided jobs to 21 million Americans, nearly one out of every seven citizens in the private sector.

Notwithstanding these impressive figures, franchising as a method of marketing and distributing products and services is appropriate only for certain kinds of companies. Despite the favorable media attention that franchising has received over the past few years as a method of business growth, it is not for everyone. A host of legal and business prerequisites must be satisfied before any company can seriously consider franchising as an alternative for rapid expansion, ranging from disclosure documents mandated by federal and state law to detailed operations manuals and marketing systems.

Intellectual capital agrarians may consider franchising as a harvesting strategy for a wide variety of reasons, ranging from capital efficiency to effective brand deployment and consumer loyalty. In many cases, the franchisee as a hands-on owner-operator with superior knowledge of the local market will outperform the salaried manager on a unit-to-unit basis. The overhead burden and headaches associated with site selection, employee hiring and firing, and customer service are shifted to the franchisee, who pays an initial franchise fee and an ongoing royalty payment for the use of the franchisor's brands, systems, and processes, as well as access to the franchiser's resources, manuals, and field support. As with any long-term and truly interdependent business relationship, the dynamics between the franchisor and franchisee must be populated with trust, integrity, innovation, mutual risk and reward, and a value proposition that may never become stale or taken for granted. The greater the levels of transparency, collaboration, and opportunities for franchisee input on new products and services, the greater the chances for the long-term sustainability and health of the franchise system. (For more information on building a franchising system and on the legal, operational, and financial aspects of franchising, see my book *Franchising and Licensing: Two Powerful Ways to Grow Your Business in Any Economy*, 4th edition [AMACOM, 2011].)

CHAPTER 9

The Global Intellectual Asset Frontier

Globalization has changed us into a company that searches the world, not just to sell or to source, but to find intellectual capital—the world's best talents and greatest ideas.

—JACK WELCH

The globalization of our economy is now a fact of life. Technological developments such as the rapid growth in the use of the Internet to facilitate international e-commerce and advances in telecommunications and videoconferencing and satellite technology have brought us all closer together. The globalization of companies and their brands, international megamergers that create large multinational companies, the economic interdependence created by a truly integrated international financial system, and the advent of strong regional associations such as the European Union, the North American Free Trade Agreement, and the Association of Southeast Asian Nations have all contributed to the need for companies of all sizes and in virtually every type of industry to be thinking in terms of global business.

Your next customer may be global, but so may be your fiercest competitor. Your best solution for outsourcing may be an overseas company, but so may be your next legal battle. Your next round of capital may come from a foreign investor, and your next hire may be a citizen of another country, triggering immigration challenges and costs. Geography no longer stands in the way of the new agrarian's aspirations, but it also no longer serves as a barrier to protect local market share. Intellectual capital leveraging strategies need to be built around a global vision—where quality, pricing, service, and distribution must be not only globally competitive but also custom-tailored to meet local requirements and market conditions.

The Global Landscape

We often forget (and underappreciate) the size and strength of the U.S. economy—even in troubling times. Although much is written about the impressive economic growth in India and China, India's economy is on a par with that of Texas, and China's economy is on a par with that of California. Per capita income for each citizen in the United States is $46,000; it recently broke the $1,000 mark in India, and China's per capita income is close to $3,600, which is more on a par with those of impoverished nations like Algeria, El Salvador, and Albania. That leaves 48 states whose GDP, productivity, and innovation stand head and shoulders above those of some of the world's fastest-growing nations.

The United States cannot become complacent. China is forecast to be the world's largest economy by as early as 2020, and, in the summer of 2010, when Tokyo announced that Japan's economy was valued at about $1.28 trillion in the second quarter, slightly below China's $1.33 trillion, China moved into second place behind the United States. Japan's economy grew 0.4 percent in the quarter, substantially less than forecast. The fact that China has succeeded in unseating Japan and, in recent years, has passed Germany, France, and Great Britain underscores its growing clout and bolsters forecasts that China will one day pass the United States as the world's biggest economy. America's gross domestic product was about $14 trillion in 2009, so China still has quite a way to go, even if the United States remains flat and complacent.

Brick Innovation Walls for the "BRICS"

Although it is well established that the BRIC nations (Brazil, Russia, India, and China) have been among the fastest growing economies over the past 10 years, how do these nations stack up when it comes to innovation? The intellectual property laws and policies of all four countries have struggled to keep pace with those of the United States and Europe in terms of protecting inventors' rights related to their innovations, enforcing rights against infringers and counterfeiters, or facilitating research and development expenditures.

In 2008, research and development spending and innovation productivity scoring by the World Economic Forum of 133 nations were as shown in Figures 9-1 and 9-2.

Figure 9-1. Research and development spending, 2008.

Country		Rank
United States		1
Finland		3
Japan		4
Germany		7
South Korea		11
Britain		15
France		18
China		26
India		30
Russia		51

Source: World Economic Forum, ``Global Competitiveness Report 2009, 10.''

Figure 9-2. Research and development spending (% of GDP, 2008 or latest available year).

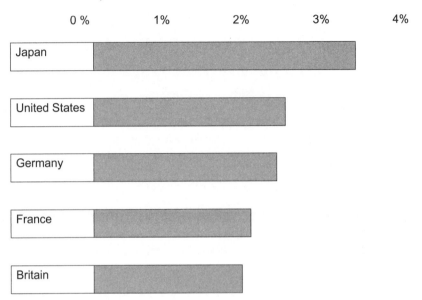

Source: Organization for Economic Cooperation and Development, Fall 2010.

The challenges transcend dollars spent on R&D. India, an economy that has been fueled by outsourcing and low-cost technology services, now publicly worries about its ability to foster homegrown innovation. The venture capital industry is considerably smaller in India than it is in the United States, and there is a cultural bias against investing in things that are unproven or that will not guarantee improved short-term gross margins. A longer-term horizon must be encouraged to foster more intellectual capital agrarianism. Indian-born inventors are every bit as educated as their global brethren, yet receive about half as many patents as are issued to companies and people in Israel and in China.

China faces its own challenges in innovation. Its economy

has been powered by a "Made in China" global manufacturing dominance as the world's largest exporter, but it lacks the development of globally recognized brands. Companies in neighboring Asian countries (Sony, Nissan, and Toyota in Japan; Samsung, Hyundai, and Kia in Korea; Acer in Taiwan; and Singapore Airlines, Tiger beer, and Creative Technologies in Singapore) have managed to capture the hearts and minds of global consumers, but can you name even one global marquee brand that has its roots in China, other than Tsingtao beer? The nation's failure to innovate leaves it reliant on stitching and welding together products that are imagined, created, and designed by others around the world.

This failure to innovate also means that Chinese companies will spend a lot more time paying licensing royalties than earning them (it was estimated that Chinese telecom manufacturers paid $100 billion in royalties to Western communications companies in 2009 alone). Small strides are being made, but mostly via mergers and acquisitions than organic innovation. In 2004, the Chinese computer manufacturer Lenovo bought IBM's laptop division for $1.25 billion, which was pretty risky, considering that the ThinkPad brand had lost $1 billion between 2000 and 2004, twice Lenovo's total profits at that time. Seven years later, in August 2010, the Chinese car manufacturer Geely bought the Volvo assets from Ford for the bargain-basement price of $1.3 billion, which was quite a deal considering that Ford had paid $6.5 billion for Volvo in 1999. In December 2010, Volvo announced plans to significantly overhaul its brand positioning and strategy, as the company was still best known for safety and for boxy cars. But buying old, tired brands and then retreating primarily back to China will not achieve the global brand domination that Apple, Nike, Coca-Cola, McDonald's, and IBM have accomplished over the years.

Intellectual Capital Agrarianism and Global Economic Development

Global attitudes toward intellectual capital and the harvesting of knowledge vary significantly around the world. Most cultures fall into one of four categories, as shown in Figure 9-3, although there are exceptions and hybrids.

The importance of effective intellectual capital harvesting strategies is being recognized by many global and country leaders around the world as a foundation for economic development. As agricultural and industrial nations join the information revolution, the creation of knowledge workers and an intellectual capi-

Figure 9-3. Intellectual capital global paradigms.

Knowledge belongs to everyone (Middle East)	Capitalistic harvesting model (U.S./parts of Europe)
Intellectual capital laws need to evolve (Latin America)	Intellectual capital rights exist but are not well enforced (parts of Asia)

tal-driven economy is now at the forefront of many political and economic agendas. From Mongolia to Ethiopia and from Chile to Iceland, country leaders are stressing the importance of intellectual capital creation, protection, and harvesting as the basis for participation and growth in the global economy. In the Middle East and North Africa (MENA) region, economic growth has fallen short of its full potential and has failed to lower the unemployment rate (which exceeds 10 percent), in part because of a failure to create knowledge workers and to seize technological development opportunities. Technology-based exports account for 25 percent to 30 percent of all exports for the MENA region, Asia, and the Pacific Rim but make up less than 1 percent of total exports from the MENA region. Some progress is being made in countries such as Egypt, Tunisia, and Jordan as they strive to harvest intellectual capital, and it is no coincidence that these nations have been among the fastest in the region to establish a middle class. In a 2010 speech, Dr. Shamshad Akhtar, the regional vice president at the World Bank for MENA, stated that the well-being of the MENA nations was directly tied to a systematic development of a knowledge-based economy. His six-part action plan included the following three elements of intellectual capital agrarianism:

1. MENA nations need to collectively launch consistent efforts to nurture industrial capabilities, and competitiveness, productivity growth, and technology absorption are essential. Besides evaluating broader trends, aligning incentive regimes at the sector and subsector levels to nurture countries' comparative advantage and competitiveness, they must encourage networked industrial structures and address intra-industry productivity differentials. These measures would induce MENA region compa-

nies to innovate by making the right investment choices and move them closer to best practices. Productivity growth and technological change need to be viewed as a means also of achieving sustainable development through a shrinking of resource and carbon footprints.

2. Human capital and the intangible assets accumulated by companies in the MENA region can foster productivity and technological change that are principal determinants of sustainable growth. There are at least four important issues that need to be addressed for MENA to be competitive as a hub of innovation: the quality of the human capital and the mix of skills; increased innovation capacity in universities and the corporate sector; integration of the business community and the education/research sector; and augmentation of the management, IT, training, and research assets of businesses.

3. Institutional development, proper governance, and implementation capacities are critical to ensuring strategic coordination on policy actions and the degree to which such coordination is reinforced by companies in the MENA region. Knowledge-based growth strategies for infusing change and effective implementation require strong coordination among different government agencies.

Stages of International Expansion

Business leaders cannot just wake up one morning and declare their businesses to be global. A strategy needs to be developed as to whether you will enter overseas markets primarily by opening offices abroad, partnering with other companies, accepting international orders from your website, or acquiring a series of overseas businesses as part of a global merger and acquisitions program. The progression toward being a truly global company usually evolves as shown in Figure 9-4.

In his book *Global Literacies* (Simon & Schuster, 2000), Dr. Robert Rosen discusses four key global literacies that a company's leadership must embrace to be successful in the adoption of a global business expansion strategy. To be a globally literate leader, an executive needs to have the personal qualities of a

Figure 9-4. Progression toward becoming a global company.

Domestic Exporter—The company operates primarily in its home country but exports its products and services abroad via e-commerce or other channels.

International Company—The company conducts marketing and production functions in both its home country and abroad, but all key management decisions are centralized in the home-country headquarters.

Multinational Enterprise—The company conducts all key business functions in multiple countries, management is decentralized, and divisions are operated and managed as truly local entities.

Global Company—The company operates in many different countries (and often several different lines of business) and is governed and structured as a truly integrated global entity.

world leader who understands and respects the challenges of doing business abroad, facilitates a level of social literacy that engages and challenges others to collaborate on a global basis, has a business literacy that focuses and mobilizes the resources of the organization toward global business objectives, and possesses a cultural literacy that includes the foresight to value and leverage the cultural differences that a global organization will face within its various business operations. *Global Literacies* and other books on this topic are an excellent starting point for understanding more about the leadership challenges that an intellectual capital agrarian will face as it seeks new globally driven harvesting opportunities.

Compliance Programs

Many U.S. and foreign laws regulate the international business activities of American companies. If your company does or plans to do business overseas, you should make sure that you have an updated compliance program to address the legal issues that arise from such activities. The adverse consequences arising from an unlawful transaction can be substantial, including revocation or suspension of export or import privileges, debarment from government contracts, negative publicity, and the expense and disruption of responding to a government investigation.

There are two categories of laws that govern the international business activities of U.S. companies. The first consists of laws that can also be applied in the domestic context, such as antitrust, employment, and economic-espionage laws. The second category consists of laws that are targeted specifically to companies that engage in international business or importing and exporting. One example is the U.S. Foreign Corrupt Practices Act (FCPA), which prohibits bribery of foreign government officials and officials of public international organizations. The scope of the FCPA can extend liability to a U.S. company based on the activities of its consultants, joint venture partners, or a recently acquired subsidiary. There are also a wide variety of controls on export and import that vary depending on the nature of the product or service and/or the specific trading partner. You should be aware of these laws and restrictions as they relate to your business in order to make sure that your company's practices are in compliance.

There are a number of ways that a company can establish and communicate standards relating to international business activities. One way is to establish a code of conduct that sets forth general policy statements regarding the company's values and objectives. This code should be distributed to all company employees, agents, and business partners. You may also choose to supplement your code of conduct with a pamphlet or an employee handbook that provides more details and identifies instances when company employees should seek further guidance from company lawyers, compliance officials, or supervisory personnel. It is important that compliance materials be carefully written to take into account the company's specific operations, practices, personnel, corporate culture, and history.

Advantages and Disadvantages of Various Forms of Doing Business Overseas

Once the decision has been made to launch an intellectual capital harvesting strategy overseas, the form of doing business is usually determined by the business objectives, available resources, and tax and legal considerations. Keep in mind, however, that no single strategy may satisfy all of your company's needs. In order to select the market entry strategy and format that are most compatible with your growth and strategic objectives, you should be familiar with the advantages and disadvantages of the principal forms of doing business overseas and the major legal issues arising from each one. They are described in the rest of this section.

Direct Exporting

* Advantages: Lower costs, and few new resources required. Complete control of operations by parent. Allows for a trial period. Reduced exposure to liability, except for product liability. Generally not subject to foreign tax, unless it is a permanent establishment.

* Disadvantages: Distance from the market; less responsive to customers' needs. Less timely service, since no one is on the scene. Less visible commitment to the market, and no local warehouse from which to meet customer emergencies.

Cooperative Relationship

* Advantages: Local presence helps foreigner learn the market and avoid mistakes that might result from ignorance of culture. Lower investment costs than forming a company.

* Disadvantages: Reduced control, and other party may have a different agenda. Not a long-term presence. Must share profits; have less control of technology.

Distributor/Sales Representative

* Advantages: Greater presence in market. Local party has greater stake and more commitment to success of business. Local inventory from which to ship goods. Lower costs and

fewer delays than are encountered by foreign companies establishing distribution network for the first time.

* Disadvantages: Must share profits with another party. Potential liability for various issues. Reduced control of distribution of products lines and chain of ownership.

Branch Office

* Advantages: Local presence with people loyal to parent company. More control over distribution network. Better commitment and faster access to market developments.

* Disadvantages: Higher costs for establishing a new office and hiring personnel. More exposure to liability due to actions of employees. Parent company is more susceptible to foreign jurisdiction in lawsuits.

Joint Venture

* Advantages: Share risks, costs, and financing. Gain knowledgeable local partner and an established presence in the market. Local partner may have complementary strengths. Allows for the establishment of business culture with an exchange of ideas.

* Disadvantages: Share profit, control, and know-how. Effort and image may be hurt by a weak local partner.

Wholly Owned Corporation

* Advantages: Complete control of profits, operations, and management. Can unilaterally withdraw if business does not succeed.

* Disadvantages: No local partner to advise on customs and culture. Greater costs and liability than when acting through an agent or with a partner. Potential start-up delays from establishing an operation in a new market.

The Most Common Mistakes When Developing an International Intellectual Capital Harvesting Strategy

Intellectual capital agrarians often make strategic and operational mistakes when first leveraging their overseas intellectual capital abroad. The most common mistakes include these:

* **Failing to obtain qualified advice.** Unless the company already has internal staff with considerable global business expertise, it is advisable to bring on consultants and advisers who can help with this process.

* **Having insufficient commitment to international business by top management.** It may take more time and effort to establish a presence in an overseas market than in domestic ones. Although the early delays and costs involved in going abroad may seem difficult to justify, the company should take a long-range view of this process and be patient in its demands for a financial return on investments.

* **Taking insufficient care in selecting overseas distributors.** The selection of each foreign distributor is crucial. The complications involved in overseas communications and transportation require that international distributors act with greater independence than their domestic counterparts. Also, since your company's history, trademarks, and reputation are usually unknown in the foreign market, foreign customers may buy on the strength of a distributor's reputation. You should therefore conduct a thorough evaluation of the personnel handling your account, the distributor's facilities, and the management methods employed.

* **Chasing orders from around the world instead of establishing a basis for profitable operations and orderly growth.** If you initially expect the partners or distributors you appoint overseas to actively promote your products and services, then these partners and distributors must be trained and assisted and their performance must be continually monitored. This requires a commitment by you to allocate staff to actively monitor and support the partners and distributors in their geographical region.

* **Neglecting overseas business when the domestic market recovers.** Too many entrepreneurs and growing companies turn to

(continues)

a global focus only when business falls off in the United States and markets abroad seem more attractive than our own. But that does not mean that a global strategy should take a back seat just because the U.S. economy begins to rebound. Such neglect can seriously harm the business and reduce the motivation of their overseas representatives, strangle the American company's own export trade, and leave the company without recourse when domestic business falls off again.

* **Assuming that a given market technique and product will automatically be successful in all countries.** What works in one market may not work in others. Each market has to be treated separately to ensure maximum success. Often, growing companies carry out institutional advertising campaigns and offer special discounts, sales incentive programs, specific credit term programs, and warranty offers in the U.S. market but fail to make similar assistance available to their international partners and distributors.

* **Being unwilling to modify products to meet regulations or cultural preferences of other countries.** Foreign distributors and market partners cannot ignore local safety and security codes and import restrictions. If necessary modifications are not made at the factory, the market partner or distributor must make them—usually at greater cost and, perhaps, not as well. It should also be noted that the resulting smaller profit margin will make the account less attractive.

CHAPTER 10

The Future of Innovation

The best way to predict the future is to invent it.
—PETER DRUCKER

As intellectual capital agrarians, we peer into the future with hope, and what do we see? We see crops that are picked on time before they rot or spoil because they are recognized as valuable and well managed. We see technological systems that facilitate and ensure collaboration in ways we could only previously have imagined. We see corporate and institutional leaders as genuine stewards of their company's intellectual assets, adopting a "no technology left behind" culture and mantra. We see internal red tape, politics, and turf wars abolished in favor of a model where institutional shareholder value is maximized and the "we" is far greater than the "me." We see companies embracing intellectual capital harvesting, leveraging, and partnering strategies at a rapid

231

pace, hungry for the new opportunities and revenue streams that will result from the fruits of their strategic labors. We see access to information being deepened, widened, and made more accessible in ways that we cannot today imagine. We see transparency, integrity, and honesty in governance and leadership, with a passionate devotion to innovation and shareholder value driving resource allocation decisions.

Is this vision for the future fantasy or reality? Luxury or necessity? Survival or death? Panacea or best practice?

You decide.

But, as of the date of this writing, what follows are my thoughts as to what the future of innovation may hold for us all.

The STEM Initiatives

On January 31, 2006, the Science, Technology, Engineering, and Mathematics (STEM) educational initiatives were launched under former president George W. Bush in response to some alarming statistics about the lack of competency and interest in science and mathematics among our nation's youth In 2005, the National Academies of Sciences (NAS) released a landmark report, "Rising Above the Gathering Storm," which stated, "The scientific and technological building blocks of America's economic leadership are eroding." According to the report, improving American students' performance in math and science coursework is the most effective way to increase the United States' global competitiveness. Recommendations outlined in the report issued by the NAS included:

* Motivating students to learn from and perform well in math and science courses

* Providing math and science teachers with professional development opportunities

* Supporting the development of highly qualified math and science teachers

The United States needs 400,000 new graduates in STEM fields by 2015. In the next 10 years, the United States will need 240,000 middle and high school math and science teachers. The initiatives were proposed to address shortfalls in federal government support of educational development and progress at all academic levels in the STEM fields. The report called for significant increases in federal funding for advanced R&D programs (including a doubling of federal funding support for advanced research in the physical sciences through the Department of Education) and an increase in the number of higher education graduates in the STEM disciplines.

In November 2009, President Barack Obama launched the "Educate to Innovate" campaign, a nationwide effort to help reach the administration's goal of moving American students from the middle of the pack to the front in science and math achievement over the next decade. The president pledged to establish a series of partnerships involving leading companies, universities, foundations, nonprofits, and organizations representing millions of scientists, engineers, and teachers that will motivate and inspire young people across the country to excel in science, technology, engineering, and mathematics.

Private sector initiatives launched in 2009 and 2010 to address this problem include:

* **National Math and Science Initiative (NMSI):** This nonprofit organization is designed to facilitate the national scale-

up of programs that have demonstrated their ability to improve students' performance in math and science education. Its primary goals include (1) developing a new generation of highly qualified math and science teachers by replicating the acclaimed Uteach program across the United States and (2) elevating student achievement by expanding AP and pre-AP courses, providing extensive training of teachers, identifying and developing "lead" teachers, and providing financial incentives based on academic results.

* **Mickelson ExxonMobil Teachers Academy:** This joint initiative between ExxonMobil and professional golfer Phil Mickelson provides third- through fifth-grade teachers with the knowledge and skills they need to motivate students to pursue careers in math and science.

* **Building a Presence for Science:** The largest initiative of the National Science Teachers Association (NSTA), with major funding provided by ExxonMobil, this program is designed to improve the teaching and learning of science for students from kindergarten through twelfth grade. The goal of the program is to provide professional development opportunities and science teaching resources built around a state coordinator, key leaders and super key leaders, and Points of Contact currently active in schools across the country. The pipeline of Gen X and Gen Y students (those ages 12 to 30) who expressed interest in this career path had dwindled to record lows, and strong concerns had been expressed concerning our nation's ability to innovate and remain competitive.

As of the fall of 2010, U.S. students ranked twenty-first in mathematics and twenty-fifth in science among secondary school children in the world's 30 most-industrialized nations. The United States ranks twelfth in college graduation rates and fifteenth in literacy rates, which is not terribly impressive for the world's largest economy. And the United States is facing problems not just in technical skills but also in language skills. Right now, there are 200 million children in China studying English and only 24,000 American children learning Chinese. Think about that for a minute as you ponder America's ability to compete in the future.

How can we establish the foundation for future technological innovation with these rankings? What steps can be taken to improve our position? In a globally integrated economy, does it really matter as long as growing and established companies have access to the resources they need? Or should the United States focus more on the types of innovation that are forward-looking in the areas of branding and marketing, financial and business models, distribution and channel partnering, human capital development, and productivity enhancement? The future of innovation will depend on the success in the implementation of these various initiatives.

Diversity and Innovation

Over the course of this book, we have learned that innovation is truly a collaborative discipline and that we have always learned and accomplished more together than alone. When building teams dedicated to the tasks of innovation, creativity, and problem solving or idea generation, a healthy dose of diversity needs to be infused, not just in the obvious categories of gender, race, religion, and age but also in talent, training, primary language, background, perspective, upbringing, nationality, sexual preference, personality type, body type, and lifestyle. Even diversity of hobbies, interests, athletic abilities, and talents can contribute to higher levels of productivity in innovation and creativity. Our society is more global and multicultural than ever, and this trend is gathering strength daily. Teams developing new products, services, and ideas must be reflective of the consumers who are being targeted. Web 2.0, collaborative networks, and crowdsourcing are all here to stay as tools for innovation, and our teams should be mirror images of the communities that we serve. For more information on the critical role and intersection between innovation and diversity, look at the work of my friend and recognized researcher Susanne Justesen, the champion and thought leader behind Innoversity (www.innoversity.org).

Faster, Better, Cheaper, Easier (FBCE) (Choose Two)

Intellectual capital agrarianism in the future will depend on innovations built on the right mix of product features and service variables aligned with market trends, as well as a genuine understanding of consumer demand. For example, medical innovation could make heart surgery more effective and more efficient, but are consumers really demanding heart surgery that is faster? Most patients already feel as though they are being rushed out of hospitals faster than makes good sense. If a doctor is working on my heart, I think my key message would be to take your time and get it right.

Consumers Know What They Want (Just Ask Them)

New agrarians are learning to truly harness the creativity of their customers and better understand their needs in real time. Look at

Zazzle's growth over the past three years. Walking a mile in the shoes of the customer or experiencing a "day in the life of _____," the target market is far more effective than suggestion boxes or even online crowdsourcing. When Doug McMillon, president and CEO of Wal-Mart International and head of its global operations, visited China in mid-2010, he didn't just visit stores; he went into the homes of Chinese consumers and visited customers to learn their needs and understand their shopping preferences. In 2010, Toyota hired InnoCentive, Inc., to support a marketing initiative that challenges consumers to come up with innovative nonautomobile applications that make use of Toyota technologies.

The Power of 80,000

Every day, 80,000 medical and biotechnology researchers go to work in search of new miracles, as well as incremental improvements in how we live, how we heal, how we cope with pain, how our ailments are treated, how we react to pharmaceuticals, how and what we eat, and how various factors motivate us to act or resist action. What can nonmedical companies lean from medical research and resource allocation decisions? In the field of biotechnology, the industry has produced more than 250 established products and vaccines that have saved the lives and improved the quality of life for millions of people around the world, with a focus on targeted therapies, antiretroviral drugs, and biotech-harvested vaccines, and there are another 600 new products in the pipeline. Around the world, more than 50 biorefineries are being built to produce cellulosic and algae biofuels, renewable chemicals and plastics, and advanced transportation fuels.

The lessons that the intellectual capital agrarian can take from the biotechnology industry concern the powers of patience and persistence and the reality that it takes money to make money. Companies can learn from the best practices of this industry, which most often must make significant capital investments and be willing to accept long-term investment horizons to achieve results that eventually both have an impact and are profitable. Real innovation does not happen overnight.

Beyond Our Field of Vision

To innovate, we must research, communicate, and collaborate differently. Focused or problem-centric research approaches can uncover new solutions to existing problems and sometimes, by accident, yield truly new discoveries, but we must redefine the scope of our creativity. If you know what you are looking for, then you are limited by what you know. We need to build more flexibility, tolerance, and support for risk taking into research budgets in the future. Our research must be more symbiotic and cross-disciplinary, as well as more open and transparent. We must be more willing to step outside our comfort zones and overcome our fears of failure, shame, or disappointment.

Spend Smarter, Not Bigger

Budgets are constrained everywhere and at every level, especially in the face of global recession. But the answer is not to spend more; it is to spend smarter. Spending on innovation is not a reliable metric for two reasons. First, things that are not directly related to innovation are lumped into the innovation budget item (e.g., patents, inventions, creativity, marketing). Second, spending by itself provides no insights into a company's innovation posture or culture or its processes for achieving future innovation success. Spending on R&D is not a reliable indicator of future innovation success, although it's often used as a leading indicator by companies, Wall Street investors, and industry observers. The number of patents held or new patents granted is also commonly used, but this is an erroneous indicator of innovation. There's an endless list of struggling companies that own thousands of patents, spend billions on R&D, and yet cannot monetize their intellectual property. Spending on product improvement is not a reliable indicator of future innovation success; for many industries, there is a negative correlated.

Top 10 Predictors of Future Innovation Success

Peter Balbus, the CEO of Pragmaxis and a thought leader on innovation and technology communications, has written that the following 10 indicators or metrics can be excellent predictors of future innovation success. On the basis of my experience in working with both rapid-growth and established companies, I agree with him whole-heartedly. His criteria are:

1. Senior management, especially the CEO, has established and articulated profitable revenue growth as the core objective for the company.
2. Specific targets are established for each operating division and for the company as a whole for how much of future revenues will come from new products and services (e.g., 30% of revenues will come from products and services introduced within the past three years).
3. Innovation and creativity are encouraged, recognized, and rewarded for all employees, regardless of their titles or job descriptions.

(continues)

4. Company policy allocates a minimum of 10 percent of each employee's time to be spent on independent thinking and innovation/creative endeavors.

5. Every employee has a personal career development plan that is regularly revisited as part of performance reviews.

6. The primary function of HR is considered to be personnel development, not administration of comp and benefits.

7. All employees must satisfy continuing-education requirements throughout their careers.

8. Managers are rotated through different disciplines over the course of their careers with the company.

9. Open innovation is the stated policy of the company.

10. There is a functional chief innovation officer (who may not necessarily have this title) and directors/VPs of innovation in every strategic business unit (SBU).

Leveling the Playing Field

For decades, patent and intellectual property litigation was referred to as the "Sport of Kings," meaning that only companies with gigantic budgets for litigation could afford to litigate against each other. In the mid-2000s, emerging private equity, venture capital, and specialty intellectual capital development and dispute funds began to back intellectual capital disputes as venture investors. Law firms responded by being more willing to take on these matters on a partial or fully contingent basis. The battleground has become more level as Davids are challenging Goliaths . . . and winning.

One of the most publicized cases was a judgment in 2006 against Research in Motion ("R.I.M.") that threatened government and business leaders with the loss of their coveted Black-Berries if the patent dispute was not settled. NTP, a David, had sued RIM and other Goliaths for patent infringement. And victorious NTP is not done yet. In July 2010, it announced that it had its eyes on more targets, including Apple, Google, Microsoft, HTC, LG, and Motorola. The lawsuits were filed in the summer of 2010 in federal district court in Richmond, Virginia, and charged that the cellphone e-mail systems of those companies are illegally using NTP's patented technology. This round of litigation against leaders in the smartphone hardware and software market is the latest step in NTP's strategy to allege that its intellectual property is the foundation of modern wireless e-mail systems. Its critics have said that NTP has consistently inflated the scope of its innovations and that NTP is the very model of a patent "troll," a company that produces no product or service other than licensing demands and lawsuits.

No matter what your opinion of NTP, clearly its success has inspired smaller companies and entrepreneurs to continue to invest precious and highly limited resources in invention and innovation, knowing that their rights can and will be protected if a large company knowingly or unknowingly trespasses on its turf. At the same time, like a new set of car keys given to a 16-year-old, these rights cannot be abused to the point of IP-ambulance chasing, which will have a dampening effect on innovation spending by larger companies. The future of innovation depends on all players in the ecosystem being committed to fair play and the reasonable enforcement of their legal rights.

The Singularity Movement and the Conveyance of Man and Machine

It may seem Orwellian to imagine a genuine conveyance of technology and the human mind, but that's exactly what the Singularity University has its sights on. Established in 2008 by leading minds such as Google co-founder Larry Page and infamous inventor Raymond Kurzweil, the university is an interdisciplinary institution whose mission is to assemble, educate, and inspire a cadre of leaders who strive to blend and facilitate the development of exponentially advancing technologies, such as biotechnology, robotics, nanotechnology, artificial intelligence, energy, and supercomputing. Executive programs focus on the intersection between the capacity of human thinking and the technology that we build in order to advance innovation and to foster mental and physical immortality.

Going Private?

Many of our largest intellectual capital-rich companies are publicly held, forcing their leaders to live and perform quarter to quarter and to meet the demands of analysts and the marketplace. The unintended consequence of this behavior is a virtual stranglehold on innovation, which by definition causes a growing chasm between the demands on a CEO and the expectations and best interests of its stockholders. The chasm is showing up in shareholders' frustration over lack of innovation. The average holding period of a NYSE-listed company in 1970 was five years; by early 2011, it was less than two months. In 1970, fewer than 10 percent of all stocks landed were done so electronically; today, more than 70 percent of all trading is driven by software programs and algorithms. Leaders of relevance-rich companies need to connect with genuine value-creation best practices if we are ever going to be capable of genuine leadership in the future.

Bigger Bang for the Taxpayer's Buck

Each year, the federal government grants or spends $150 billion in R&D. No reliable data exist or measure what happens from there. Intellectual capital agrarians driving the future of innovation must develop systems for measuring the results of this spending and foster stronger best practices and processes for harvesting and communicating the crops from this annual harvest.

The federal government is experimenting with a wide variety of other ways to foster innovation and entrepreneurship, as well. At the end of the 111th Congress, the reauthorization of the "America Competes Act" (full name: the "America Creating Opportunities to Meaningfully Promote Excellence in Technology, Education, and Science Act") overhauled the way the federal government supports private-sector research and development. One of the main ways the government hopes to support R&D is with prizes and project-specific awards. Such "inducement prizes" (as opposed to "recognition prizes," like the Nobel or the MacArthur or the Pulitzer) are a critical component of the Obama administration's Strategy for American Innovation.

Can government-granted prizes and recognition really work to stimulate innovation? There is some history to support this premise. Most famously, in 1714, the British government offered 20,000 pounds to anyone who could devise a reliable way of measuring longitude at sea, a problem neither Newton nor Galileo could solve, but clockmaker John Harrison accomplished it in 1773. At the turn of the nineteenth century, Napoleon offered a prize for innovations in food preservation for his French army, and this led to the development of modern canning. And, in 1919, the $25,000 Orteig Prize, offered by New York hotel owner Raymond Orteig to the first allied aviator to fly nonstop from New York City to Paris, inspired Charles Lindbergh to make his first transatlantic flight. The Orteig Prize was to inspire the Ansari X Prize, created in 1996 for advances in commercial spaceflight.

Does Size Really Matter?

Small companies innovate to survive and large companies innovate to compete, but what about the country's middle-market companies? Politicians love to talk about initiatives to protect small business and offer incentives and olive branches to our global conglomerates, but nobody seems to want to engage in a dialogue to create incentives for middle-market companies, which are often too big to be small and too small to be big. Our nation's middle-market companies offer significant kinetic potential to contribute to the base of innovation and creativity and to make excellent joint-venture and strategic-alliance partners to both their smaller and larger counterparts as both mentor and mentee. The future of innovation will depend on a meaningful and productive dialogue with the leaders of these companies to develop incentives and rewards for investment in R&D and job creation by this important segment of our economy, which usually gets lost in the political shuffle.

If You Want Big Ideas, Go to Where the Big Brains Live

We are the leading nation of globally respected universities by far. More than 80 percent of the world's most respected top 50 universities are in the United States. A recent study found that Massachusetts Institute of Technology alumni, faculty, and staff have founded more than 4,000 companies during the past four decades, employing more than 1.1 million people and having annual world sales of $232 billion. Most of these companies are knowledge based. This emphasizes the necessity for keeping research universities strong to maintain a high level of innovation. They provide the scientific workforce of the future and are the source of most of the research that drives major innovation; young people with new ideas start many new companies after leaving the university.

We also need to learn to replicate and expand the success of our regional ecosystems. In a country where we are still the best in the world of innovation and creativity, why are the same cities—Austin, Boston, D.C., and Palo Alto—mentioned over and over again as the best places for birthing new technologies? The future of innovation in America should include 40 successful technological centers of influence, not 4! However, there have been a few surprises on that front in recent years. In a 2010 study by the Kauffman Foundation, Utah was the most innovative state, at 22.1 patents per million people. Why? Because Utah offers low taxes, minimal business regulations, and an innovative program, called the Utah Science Technology and Research (UTAR) initiative, which offers grants to build commercialization bridges between entrepreneurs and state universities. The second most innovative state was Oregon (14.4 patents per million), which has a young and highly educated population with a pioneering lifestyle and culture. The rest of the top 5 were California (11.3), Massachusetts (9.8), and Connecticut (9.4).

Learning from Our Agrarian Brethren

We may have graduated from an agrarian society many decades ago, but we can still learn from current technological developments in today's farming and agricultural communities. New agrarians must look at new venues, business models, efficiencies, and eco-friendly designs as part of their foundation and strategies for innovation and growth in the future. For example, new developments in urban farming offer insights on new ways to utilize open space, foster community development, and solve distribution inefficiencies, among other issues. Urban agriculture is not limited to fruits and vegetables; it has expanded to include innovative forms of animal husbandry, aquaculture, agroforestry, and horticulture. It has been estimated that as much as 20 percent of America's food supply by 2018 could come from rooftops, parking lots, and other urban farming strategies. (Discussions about home farms, microfarms, urban farming trends, agricultural developments, pioneers, and supporters can be found at www.urbanfarming.org.)

The latest trend is "vertical farming," which builds food towers on a vertical, space/land-efficient basis in the most unlikely spaces, such as along the outdoor and indoor walls of skyscrapers. Pioneer and thought leader Dickson Despommier challenges the notion that crops should be grown in horizontal soil; he suggests using hydroponic greenhouses and other indoor growing technologies that use less (or even no) herbicides, pesticides, or fertilizers. (For more information, visit www.verticalfarm.com.) Jim Mumford, a visionary entrepreneur in the gardening and horticultural industries and founder of Good Earth Plant and Flower Company in San Diego, developed the concept of "Edible Walls," functional outdoor walls made from modular boxes that can be seeded and harvested just like a horizontal garden but are much more space-efficient, especially in expensive urban areas. One of Mumford's customers has an edible wall separating his two restaurants in West Hollywood; not only is the wall attractive, but it also yields 324 plants producing key ingredients used in the restaurants, including herbs, such as mint, chicory, rosemary, and sage, and vegetables, such as beets.

Head in the Clouds

Our ability to conduct complex research in a wide variety of industries has been facilitated by cloud computing and will only continue to improve as the technology evolves. The power of cloud computing should help close the critical gap between R&D dollars spent and the measurable and useful outputs of these critical dollars and resources. The ability to pool and share computing resources and storage on an "as needed" and "pay as you go" basis will help facilitate research that might have taken months or years in the past but that will now be accomplished in a matter of days or hours. It can also significantly reduce the costs of R&D. Offering convenience of access and greatly enhanced opportunities for global-scale collaboration, this breakthrough should help make research more productive and efficient. The ability to juxtapose large quantities of information and search the data for new insights and linkages will help power breakthroughs in pharmaceutical research, macroeconomic forecasting, alternative energy, and robotics. The missing glue that will evolve over time are the gatekeeping and orchestration services around cloud computing that will manage user access, reliability, security, and validation.

Web 3.0 by 2013

From 1997 to 2003, we were all enthralled by the connectivity of Web 1.0. Starting in 2003, the connectivity of Web 1.0 was replaced by interactivity and social networking offered by Web 2.0 developments as one-to-one became one-to-many. By 2013, we will start feeling the effects of Web 3.0, which will feature advances in productivity (smartphone applications performing functions to help us in our business and personal lives in ways we can't imagine today), as well as technologies, such as holography, biometrics, nanotechnology, and robotics, which will all influence visual collaboration, enable smarter and faster computing and wider and deeper Web search capabilities, and power enhanced data management, advanced diagnostics, and more reliable communications.

As we peer into the future, we cannot forget the past, nor must all of the most useful innovation come from truly new ideas or vision. Sometimes the most obvious innovation or inventions are sitting right under our noses if we would just take the time to breathe them in. This was the case with something that practically all of us use today when we travel—the rolling luggage suitcase. Although both the wheel and the sack were invented thousands of years ago and used in many ways and in many different industries, it took visionaries and inventors in the 1970s and 1980s like tourist Bernard Sadow and pilot Robert Plath to develop applications of rolling luggage that were initially used primarily by flight crews and eventually made their way into the closets of every family around the world that goes on vacation and every business traveler who must deal with an overnighter.

Some of the best intellectual capital agrarianism can be accomplished with fields, tools, fertilizers, and workers that are already in place in your company—if you have the vision and take the time to put the puzzle pieces together, empower them with the authenticity and the resources to plant the seeds, and establish the structures and the channels to harvest the crops.

Innovation has been part of the fabric of our society since its inception and is part of the heart of our nation's charter. A few observations from some of America's greatest leaders of the past capture it best—the future of innovation rests in all of our hearts, our minds, our spirit, and our grit. We strive to evolve and to make the world a better place in our quest for creativity and the advancement of mankind.

The dogmas of the quiet past are inadequate to the stormy present. The occasion is piled high with difficulty, and we must rise—with the occasion. As our case is new, so we must think anew, and act anew. We must disenthrall ourselves, and then we shall save our country.
—Abraham Lincoln

Some men look at things the way they are and ask why? I dream of things that are not and ask why not?
—Robert Kennedy

For this is what America is all about. It is the uncrossed desert and the unclimbed ridge. It is the star that is not reached and the harvest that is sleeping in the unplowed ground.
—Lyndon B. Johnson

APPENDIX

Directory of Licensing Resources, Exchanges, and Agents

This appendix contains some additional resources and organizations that may be useful in your quest to commit to being an intellectual capital agrarian.

Organizations Focused on Fostering Fair Practices Relating to IP:

* **The World Intellectual Property Organization** (www.wipo.int) is a specialized agency of the United Nations. One of WIPO's principal objectives is to promote synchronized laws and practices regarding IP among its member states. Another core task for WIPO is to help protect IP by allowing

251

members to file for international patents and trademarks as well as by offering arbitration and mediation to individuals and businesses in order to resolve IP disputes. WIPO has a free online database that allows users to search for IP data.

* **The International Trademark Association** (www.inta.org) is a not-for-profit membership association dedicated to the support and advancement of trademarks and related intellectual property as elements of fair and effective commerce. INTA supports its network of 5,700 trademark owners by advocating for effective and harmonized international trademark laws. INTA's website provides resources for researching trademark law and initiatives.

* **Licensing Executives Society International** (www.lesi.org) is an association of 32 national and regional societies that focuses on transfer of technology and licensing of intellectual property rights. LESI has more than 10,000 individual members, including representatives of companies, scientists, engineers, academicians, governmental officials, lawyers, patent and trademark attorneys, and consultants. A core LESI objective is to encourage professional standards among individuals engaged in the transfer and licensing of technology and industrial or intellectual property rights. LESI assists members in improving their skills in the licensing trade. LESI sponsors educational meetings and publishes reports and articles relating to licensing.

* **The American Intellectual Property Law Association** (www.aipla.org) is a national bar association constituted primarily of lawyers in private and corporate practice, in government service, and in the academic community. AIPLA produces a number of informative publications pertaining to IP law. AIPLA is also actively involved in shaping U.S. intellectual property pol-

icy and has started a worldwide campaign to reduce the costs of procurement and enforcement of patents and trademarks.

* **The National Inventor Fraud Center** (www.inventor-fraud
.com) has as its objective to provide consumers with information about invention promotion and how to market ideas without falling victim to companies that sell the marketing of inventions but do not realize any results for the inventors.

* **National Research Council Canada** (www.nrc-cnrc.gc
.ca) is an organization of the Government of Canada. NRC has more than 20 institutes and programs that offer services in various areas of science and technology. NRC seeks to develop partnerships with private- and public-sector organizations in Canada and around the world in order to create technology and foster wealth creation.

IP Research Sources:

* **Community of Science** (www.cos.com) offers memberships to individual researchers and universities. Membership allows researchers to search a database for funding opportunities, including grants and sponsorships for research and scholarship. Through COS, researchers can find collaborators for their projects. COS offers memberships to corporations so that they can find collaborators and assess their R&D projects.

* **RefAware** (www.refaware.com) is a Web-based service that monitors the Internet in order to provide its members with updates of peer-reviewed and non-refereed sources of information shortly after they are posted online. Users can create distinct searches in order to track new developments in their area of interest.

Appendix ✿

Online Licensing Exchanges:

Note: Licensing exchanges serve as electronic marketplaces linking licensors and licensees. Some of these websites also act as "offline" licensing agents and consultants, as well as exchanges.

* **The iBridge Network** (www.ibridgenetwork.org) is a program of the not-for-profit Kauffman Innovation Network, Inc. Membership in iBridge allows the user to search for early-stage inventions that have been posted to the iBridge site by researchers at universities.

* **TechTransferOnline.com** (www.techtransferonline.com) is an online exchange where users can post and search for IP. The website also facilitates secure sales and licensing of IP.

* **PriorIp** (www.prior-ip.com) is a research tool that uses sophisticated algorithms to cluster innovations and patent applications. This clustering allows for the user to find patent information and then easily find related patents.

* **Yet2.com** (www.yet2.com) provides an online source where IP owners can post their IP to a searchable database. Yet2.com also provides a marketplace where its members can license and sell IP.

* **Flintbox** (www.flintbox.com) is a platform for universities, corporations, entrepreneurs, and technology communities to seek out collaborators for their own innovations or find innovations on which they want to participate.

* **Knowledge Express** (www.knowledgeexpress.com) offers subscriptions to its searchable databases, which provide coverage of agreements, corporate profiles, clinical trials, deals, drug pipelines, drug sales, licensable technologies, patents, and royalty rates.

Patent Brokers:

Note: These companies can assist in the sale of intellectual assets.

   * **Ocean Tomo's Private IP Brokerage** (www.ocean tomo.com) practice consists of providing advisory services for intellectual property transactions.

   * **ThinkFire** (www.thinkfire.com) assists patent owners who wish to sell underutilized or redundant parts of their patent portfolios.

Patent Auctions:

   * **ipauctions** (www.ipauctions.com) is an online market-place where ownership of IP is auctioned off to the highest bidder.

   * **ICAP Ocean Tomo** (www.icapoceantomo.com) holds live IP auctions in specified locations and at specified times.

Direct Licensing Firms:

Note: These companies will directly acquire or fund your IP and seek to license it and/or enforce it themselves.

   * **Acacia Technologies LLC** (Nasdaq: ACTG) (http://acaciatechnologies.com) is engaged in the business of acquiring patent rights for licensing and enforcement. Acacia becomes the owner or exclusive licensee of the patent portfolio and enforces the IP rights, giving their clients a percentage of the recovery.

* **General Patent Corporation** (www.generalpatent
.com) litigates against corporations that have infringed on IP
rights of owners who cannot afford to pursue litigation on their
own. General Patent Corporation works on a contingency-fee
basis.

R&D Licensing Companies:

Note: These companies are focused on highly specific industries
and will license your IP from you, conduct R&D, and then incor-
porate the IP into their own products and technologies, which
they then license and sell.

* **MOSAID Technologies, Inc.** (TSE: MSD) (www
.mosaid.com) is an IP company focused on the licensing and
development of semiconductor and communications technologies. Mosaid's core business is the licensing of patented semiconductor and communications IP. A key to Mosaid's strategy is to
expand its patent portfolio through licensing partnerships and
patent acquisitions.

* **Tessera Technologies, Inc.** (Nasdaq: TSRA) (www
.tessera.com) licenses and delivers innovative miniaturization
technologies that transform next-generation electronic devices.
Tessera invests in and develops this technology.

Patent and IP Buyers:

Note: These companies will purchase your IP directly from you.

* **Intellectual Ventures** (www.intellectualventures.com)
uses a business model that centers on creating, acquiring, and
licensing invention in a variety of technology areas. IV commer-

cializes inventions through licensing, spin-offs, joint ventures, and industry partnerships.

* **Allied Security Trust** (AST) (www.alliedsecuritytrust .com) is a Delaware statutory trust that was originally formed by several high-technology companies to obtain cost-effective patent licenses. The Trust provides opportunities to enhance companies' freedom to sell products by sharing the cost of patent licenses. The Trust creates new opportunities for patent holders.

* **RPX Corporation** (www.rpxcorp.com) acquires patent rights that could be used against its members in patent enforcement litigation. The RPX Defensive Patent Aggregation does not require member involvement in acquisitions, and RPX will not enforce the patents it purchases.

Spin-Out Financing Sources:

Note: These companies invest in companies that develop IP that has been created by corporate research and design departments but not pursued. Corporate IP spin-outs cut down on the high expense of IP development.

* **Blueprint Ventures** (www.blueprintventures.com) is a technology investment firm that specializes in corporate spin-out IP.

* **New Venture Partners** (www.nvpllc.com) uses a business model that seeks to establish close, long-term relationships with global technology corporations to commercialize innovations through spin-out ventures. NVP identifies, develops, and funds its clients' IP in order to create stand-alone companies, transforming technologies from corporate R&D labs into successful spin-outs.

Appendix

Mature company investors/litigation financing:

Note: Mature companies with strong IP can get capital and/or litigation financing from these firms.

* **Altitude Capital Partners** (www.altitudecp.com) invests in businesses that own intellectual property assets. Altitude invests common equity, preferred stock, subordinated, or secured debt to fund capital for organic growth, acquisitions, strategic IP licensing and litigation activities, or to facilitate distributions to existing shareholders.

IP holders who believe their patents are being infringed can get infringement litigation funding from these firms:

* **Rembrandt** (www.rembrandtip.com) provides capital and strategic advice to companies, individuals, universities, and investors with strong IP in order to enforce their rights against companies that are infringing upon that IP.

* **NW Patent Funding Corporation** (www.nwpatent-funding.com) partners with owners of IP to create new licensing programs from dormant or underutilized IP. NW contributes funding and management, and royalties from the licensing programs are split between NW and the IP owners.

Intellectual Property Exchanges:

* **Intellectual Property Exchange International** (www.ipxi.com) provides a marketplace for trading IP rights. Owners of IP can use IPXI to find a price. IPXI adheres to a policy of not infringing on IP owners' rights. The exchange uses input from leading corporate IP owners in order to provide a fair and reasonable price for IP.

Index

Index   ✤

Index

Index

Index